There is a garden in every childhood, an enchanted place where colors are brighter, the air softer, and the morning more fragrant than ever again.

Elizabeth Lawrence

LEARNING **BY DESIGN**
LIVE | PLAY | ENGAGE | CREATE

Prakash Nair & Roni Zimmer Doctori
with
Dr. Richard F. Elmore
Professor Emeritus, Harvard University

Foreword by
Dr. Heidi Hayes Jacobs
Author, Curriculum 21 and Bold Moves

Education Design International

Education Design International, USA

Learning by Design: Live | Play | Engage | Create

Architecture/Education/School Reform

Copyright 2019/2020 © Education Design International, Prakash Nair, Roni Zimmer Doctori, Richard Elmore

ISBN 978-0-9762670-6-5

The copyright holders hereby grant the holder of this book limited permission to photocopy selections from this copyrighted publication for nonprofit and educational use subject to the following conditions: 1. Photocopies must include a statement that the material is copied from Learning by Design © 2019 Education Design International, Prakash Nair, Roni Zimmer Doctori and Richard F. Elmore and 2. Photocopies must include any other credit and/or copyright notice applicable to the material copied. Reproduction or storage in any form of electronic retrieval system for any commercial purpose is prohibited without the express written permission of the copyright holder. All rights reserved.

Editor: Pam Sampson

Cover Design: Dmytro Zaporozhtsev

Book Design: Dmytro Zaporozhtsev

Illustrations: Kristie Anderson

Graphic Design: Bruce Johnson

Website: LearningByDesign.co

A majority of the schools featured in this book were led by Prakash Nair, AIA while he served as President & CEO of Fielding Nair International which was reorganized in 2019. Prakash Nair now serves as President & CEO of Education Design International. Learn more about these projects at EducationDesign.com.

Front Cover Photo: Learning Community at Renovated Middle School. Academy of the Holy Names, Tampa, Florida.

Back Cover Photo: Exterior View of Meadowlark School, Erie, Colorado. Boulder Valley School District

Photo by Fred J. Fuhrmeister

CONTENTS

Foreword by Heidi Hayes Jacobs 1

PART ONE

Introduction: Back to the Future 3
Chapter One: The Educational Underpinning for Good Space Design 17
Chapter Two: Eight Principles that Define the New School Design Paradigm .. 29
Chapter Three: Live 40
Chapter Four: Play 51
Chapter Five: Engage 58
Chapter Six: Create 70
Chapter Seven: How To Transform 84
Chapter Eight: Pathfinders — Taking The First Step 105
Chapter Nine: Scaling Up Change — The Story of Boulder Valley Schools 117
Chapter Ten: New Directions for a New World 133

PART TWO

Chapter Eleven: The Challenges of Learning and Design 160

Acknowledgements 196
About the Authors 200
Design Credits 204

PART I

FOREWORD
HEIDI HAYES JACOBS

"We are architects! We are educators!" Proclaimed with conviction and experience, Prakash Nair and Roni Zimmer Doctori declare they are bringing their perspectives both as designers and specialists to the book in your hands, Learning by Design. With enthusiasm, pragmatism, and imagination, Nair and Doctori take the reader on a rewarding dive into exploring possibilities for the contemporary learner. They encourage us to envision what modern learning can and should look like in a reimagined school environment.

Given the authors' exceptional expertise as architects, it is refreshing to see their design thinking and experience reflected in the layout of the book. They set the stage with an overview of what constitutes good space design followed by the exploration of a powerful set of four shifts that guide us to considering a new school design paradigm:

- Teacher Practice: From Solo to Collaborative Teams
- Pedagogy: From Teacher Directed to Student Directed
- Curriculum: From Segregated Subjects to Interdisciplinary Courses
- Community: From Classroom to Network

These shifts move the reader to consider the world of the learner as we proceed. What I found particularly refreshing was the authors' focus on bringing a kind of natural ease to our work in schools; that is, to build on our innate desire and capacity to learn as human beings. They note that we are "learning organisms and do not need to be taught how to learn." With that concept in mind, Nair and Doctori wrap their vision around four accessible and natural elements: Live, Play, Engage, Create. We examine how to operationalize each of these fundamental tenets into curriculum and instruction planning. How to cultivate living, playing, engagement, and creation in the world of our children and young people is at the heart of this book. Their approach is to provide examples and accessible lists unpacking the four elements with succinct descriptions. We see how every decision from games, to socializing, to eating, to gardening, and on to scholarly pursuits should emerge from the four elements and tap into the motivation of our students.

The elements are followed by a direct and engaging examination of how to make the transformation happen in a setting (perhaps your setting). With a crisp and insightful review of the historical context for the development of school life in the United States, we are reminded that things have stayed remarkably the same for over a century. The time is ripe for growth and seismic change. We are encouraged as progressive educators to bring fresh thinking to the planning table. Nair and Doctori model that bold notion as they propose we consider ideas such as capital spending as a catalyst for change. They consider how this transformation can play out in steps through a systemic process engaging the "right people on the bus" that explore, research, and discover new options for consideration. We see that a master strategic plan that dynamically embraces the full array of education planning from fundamental structures to curriculum planning needs to be interconnected. What struck me as exciting was to return to the earlier chapters and see how Live, Play, Engage, Create could and should directly inform each component in a strategic plan. Over time, the authors see how implementation is gradual but steady and needs corresponding changes

> How to cultivate living, playing, engagement, and creation in the world of our children and young people is at the heart of this book.

> Elmore shines light on how our calcified views of education are loosened when we "reverse the relationship between schooling and learning."

in governance and management. This latter point is amplified in the authors' spirited chapter on Pathfinders.

Providing examples from a range of schools, Nair and Doctori take us on a kind of tour through the lens of a set of questions regarding what is happening in real settings. What is a flexible learning environment? How does it affect learning? This discrete focus on fundamental decisions regarding how we group learners, structure their time, while connecting them with flexible spaces brings all of the previous chapters together. We see that it is possible to modernize schools and to respect our learners. The case studies they provide give hope and inspiration to readers.

But, there is more. In an original and engaging book design move, Nair and Doctori invited an internationally respected colleague and one of our seminal thinkers in education, Dr. Richard F. Elmore, to provide a powerful coda to the book. His chapter, The Challenges of Learning and Design, takes us into operationalizing the potential of "learning organizations." Elmore organizes his discussion around five key propositions, a quadrant framework for analyzing the modalities and context for learning, and then provides us with a dynamic set of design principles to underscore the planning process Nair and Doctori proposed earlier in the book. Written with a deft touch, Elmore shines light on how our calcified views of education are loosened when we "reverse the relationship between schooling and learning." His contribution has gravitas, adding depth to the discussion even as it is eye-opening and engaging.

We have an exuberant and practical guide in our hands with Learning by Design, which gives educators, communities, and learners an inspired roadmap to transformation. Yes, we are all architects! We are all educators!

INTRODUCTION
BACK TO THE FUTURE

It is self-evident that the original purpose of school as a place to deliver content and knowledge ceased to apply ever since the Internet became an integral and irreversible part of our existence. How can one teacher delivering content to a diverse group of children ever compete with the personal and highly customized learning from world-renowned experts that anyone can access online? If teaching generic "stuff" is no longer the primary reason for a school's existence, then what is? Why do we need schools when their very mission has become irrelevant? This is a rhetorical question because it is an undeniable truth that given the way society is structured, only a small fraction of parents can afford to keep children at home, away from schools. The vast majority still need a place for children to be during the day when they (the parents) are at work.

That means the school continues to have a place in modern society at least in this one aspect – as a custodial service for children. This begs the question: If we have them here anyway, what kind of a place can schools be where children can be

Figure I-1: *Children are not little adults. A school's primary job is to provide opportunities for students to discover the world around them. Happy, engaged students will leave school with the skills needed to live happy, fulfilled lives.*

INTRODUCTION BACK TO THE FUTURE

Figure I-2: The "capacity" for learning starts with one key ingredient – curiosity. The learning environment should provide lots of opportunities for children to indulge their curiosity.
Early Childhood Center at Shorecrest Prep School in St. Petersburg, Florida.

children? Everything we now know about human development points to one simple fact – children are not little adults. Schools shouldn't only be about preparing children for life because, at least as far as the children are concerned, the school is their life in the here and now. As adults, we need to make this life, the one they are living every day in school, as good as it can be. This does not require us to choose between a path that makes them happy today versus one that will make them successful tomorrow. The good news is that happy, engaged students will leave school with the skills needed to live happy, fulfilled lives as productive members of society.

One of the most interesting findings of neuroscience is that learning is <u>not</u> what happens as a direct result of teaching. According to this book's distinguished co-author, Harvard Prof. Richard Elmore, "Learning is the capacity to consciously modify understandings, attitudes, and beliefs in the presence of experience and knowledge over time." The "capacity" for learning starts with one key ingredient – curiosity. Curiosity drives students to "consciously modify understandings, attitudes and beliefs." Students will only modify their existing worldviews when they are 1) convinced that there is another, more credible perspective of a particular subject or event and 2) curious and motivated enough to know what that alternative view might be. It is up to us as adults to create the conditions that lead children to ask questions and

> If teaching generic "stuff" is no longer the primary reason for a school's existence, then what is?

Figure I-3: *From a very early age, doing is the most effective form of learning. No matter how young they are, children thrive on being given meaningful tasks to complete. Working alongside expert adults as their "interns" provides motivation for students to master the craft.*

give them the freedom to explore the world around them so that they can find their own answers.

Back to the Future

The schools we are arguing for in this book are not some brand new invention. They represent the way learning used to happen before the model that we now know as "school" was invented. The predominant "cells and bells" model of school (students start the school day in a cell and move to another, identical cell when the bell goes off) that most of us are familiar with is actually a remnant of the industrial revolution. It represents the idea that education can be mass produced in a factory-like setting to churn out "educated" students ready to tackle college and careers. Of course, we now know that this model is fundamentally flawed because no two students are the same and, therefore, subjecting them to the same "process" is unlikely to yield the same result. This failing of the dominant educational model was not as apparent when the vast majority of high school graduates had factory jobs waiting for them when they graduated. These jobs

> The schools we are arguing for in this book are not some brand new invention. They represent the way learning used to happen before the model that we now know as "school" was invented.

INTRODUCTION BACK TO THE FUTURE

Figure I-4: *The traditional classroom is the building block of the "cells and bells" model of education. It has some fundamental flaws as a place for modern education starting with the fact that it severely limits the modalities of learning that students can experience since it is optimized for teacher-led direct instruction.*

needed very basic entry-level skills, and employers benefited from having a barely literate but compliant workforce. The world where high school graduates could expect employment in decent-paying factory jobs does not exist anymore. The imperative to retool schools has never been greater.

As it turns out, we are talking about a new model that actually looks a lot like one that had existed for several hundred years before the factory model school was invented — interns learning a craft from a master teacher. We will be showcasing this model in greater detail in this book. In this sense we are returning to a model where learning represents the acquisition, demonstration, and mastery of real, practical and tangible skills.

Learning by Design

The title of this book, "Learning by Design" has two key themes - Learning and Design. The word "design" represents the physical design of schools but is also meant to be read as "intent." We have to be "intentional" regarding the future of education and then put in place all the various elements that are needed to realize this intention. For us, there is no question that the most visible, and maybe even the most influential, element of the educational experience is the environment in which we place children in their most impressionable and formative years. The way a school is setup with groups of children shut in with a teacher in a classroom speaks volumes about our expectations from school. We assert that the physical school already precludes almost all the learning goals that educators claim they want for our children. Take just two words - personalization and collaboration. A classroom is the worst place to personalize education or collaborate with your peers. And when these terms are extended to include teachers, then the abject hopelessness of the classroom-based model of school becomes even more apparent.

> The most visible, and maybe even the most influential, element of the educational experience is the environment in which we place children in their most impressionable and formative years.

INTRODUCTION BACK TO THE FUTURE

No matter how well it has or has not succeeded in the past, the educational establishment has always maintained that it exists to best serve the learning needs of children and young adults so that they can become productive members of society. However, like any other large enterprise, education also has a vast array of specialists, all of whom, supposedly, are pulling in the same direction. Among education's many specialists are architects whose role is to create the environments within which everything and everyone within the world of education reside.

> The world where high school graduates could expect employment in decent-paying factory jobs does not exist anymore. The imperative to retool schools has never been greater.

Even the most rudimentary Internet research about learning and the brain, especially in the context of a rapidly changing world, tells us that we need a radical rethinking about how to educate children. Since spaces are the "container" within which any new model of education must work, we felt that it is imperative we have some understanding of this whole new world of "learning research" and neurology. That is why we reached out to the pre-eminent educational authority on this subject — Dr. Richard Elmore, professor emeritus at Harvard University. You will find his ideas embedded throughout the first part of this book, which is presented from the perspective of space design. The ideas that underpin the future of education and how we can be "intentional" about where to go from here are spelled out elegantly by Prof. Elmore in Part Two of this book.

When we think about the "space" that students need for real learning to happen, we are also referring to the social, emotional, and creative space children (of all ages) need to grow and thrive. This kind of "space for learning" is at a premium in schools. We believe that the design of the physical environment of schools can make this other "space" — the social, emotional and creative space — not only more visible, but also more available. Of course, the design itself can only do so much. For students to truly feel that they have space for learning, schools need to use the design of the physical environment as a catalyst to change the whole dynamic of a school from a teacher-centered to a student-centered place. This is the area that will benefit the most from Part Two of the book that is presented from an educator's perspective.

Figure I-5: *When we talk about "space" for learning, we are also talking about giving students the space to develop socially, emotionally and creatively. Outdoor Café at Learning Gate Community School, Lutz, Florida.*

INTRODUCTION BACK TO THE FUTURE

The transformation of a school from a teacher-centered to student-centered model will impact its curriculum, pedagogy, schedule and student assessment, not to mention its administration, operations and governance. Support systems need to be in place for this kind of a transformation that may seem radical at first but more natural as time goes on. In this

> Throughout this book, we have relied on what educators and students have told us to talk about the effectiveness of the physical spaces they inhabit.

book, in Part Two, you will start to learn about the conditions for success that need to be in place in these other areas beyond the physical design of the school campus. Prof. Elmore's section is not intended to be a how-to "manual" on education in the way that Part One may be for physical design. We have a higher purpose for his portion of the book. In reading what he has to say, we hope, our readers will understand the imperative for a holistic approach that is needed when we are talking about transforming education — and school design itself, while it is a vital part of that equation, is still only one piece of the puzzle.

Educator and Student Voices

Throughout this book, we have relied on what educators and students have told us to talk about the effectiveness of the physical spaces they inhabit. We as architects envision the ways in which the spaces we design will be used but, over time, we have learned that the actual use of spaces varies greatly from what we had anticipated. By hearing what teachers and students say about their own experiences in their learning environments, we have learned how to create living buildings that will flex and adapt to the constantly changing needs of schools. As we understand the profound impact of space not only on teaching and learning but on the overall development of young adults, we are humbled and honored to have a small role as the "architects" of student lives and not just of their learning spaces. We hope this book will be a reminder to everyone involved in the creation of school facilities of the awesome influence that physical environments wield over the lives of tens of thousands of students in the 30, 50, or even 100 years they will be in existence.

Structure of the Book

The more we talked to Dr. Elmore, the more we realized his unfiltered ideas and views deserved to be heard by our readers. This book did not start out as having two distinct parts to it but, after we read what he had to offer, we realized Dr. Elmore's thesis had to be presented in its original form and separate from our architecture-themed discussion about school design. The key principles he outlines that have directly influenced our thinking about how to structure the architectural portion of this book are summarized below in Dr. Elmore's own words.[1]

1. **Human beings are learning organisms and do not need to be taught how to learn:** We need to move away from attainment-driven models of schooling that disable human beings as learners by convincing them that they do not have the capability to manage their own learning.

2. **Individual variability is the rule, standardization is the exception:** New designs will have to take their point of departure from the assumption that individuals — children and adults — come to the learning project from different points of origin developmentally and experientially.

3. **Knowledge equals information plus affect plus cognition plus fluency:** Fluent and powerful learners tend to be highly variable in their absorptive capacity, depending on how interested they are in the knowledge they confront, how

---

[1] Excerpted from Part Two of this Book, "Learning and Design" by Dr. Richard F. Elmore, Prof. Emeritus, Harvard University

the knowledge domain matches their previous experience as learners, and how well they can use the skills of their previous learning to solve the puzzles of acquiring new knowledge.

4. **Depth and continuity over coverage:** One day, when I was 27 years old, in graduate school at Harvard, I walked out of an econometrics lecture on some hopelessly obscure topic I can't recall, and I approached one of those incredibly complicated traffic intersections near Harvard Square. It suddenly occurred to me with an electric jolt, as I observed the drivers orchestrating their behavior through the intersection, that "math is everywhere!" I realized that I could actually build a model using the language of mathematics that would describe what I was seeing.

> Teachers can be coaches, they can be counselors, and they can be role models for great learning.

5. **Learning and Design — Hard Questions, Provisional Answers:** Ambitious ventures in uncertain times begin with hard questions rather than clear answers.

   a. How will humans adapt to transformations in the practice of learning?
   b. How will the practice of learning and the design of learning environments adapt to the democratization of expertise?

Figure I-6: *Schools need to start with the assumption that all students, regardless of their age, are capable of learning and managing their own learning. For effective student-centered learning, the architecture of space, time, curriculum and the relationship between teachers and students must change.*
Meadowlark School, Boulder Valley, Colorado.
Photo © Fred J. Fuhrmeister.

INTRODUCTION BACK TO THE FUTURE

c. How will society orchestrate its duty of care and responsibility for socialization of children and adolescents with the unfreezing of institutionalized learning?
d. How will learning environments adapt to the challenges of individualization?

> "Learning" itself is a collateral activity and one that is always happening no matter what we are doing.

These ideas started to make sense to us in the context of our own lives and careers and the educational experiences of our own children. We thought about all the learning that happened outside school that so greatly impacted who we and they (our children) are today as people. Even at school, it seemed that the spaces between classes, the stolen moments away from the direct instruction of teachers, and the time spent with friends were the most important and meaningful memories we retained from our school days. As we looked at the research we realized that these peripheral experiences – all the stuff beyond the classroom – is actually where the most meaningful and long-lasting "learning" happens. In other words, "learning" itself is a collateral activity and one that is always happening no matter what we are doing. This is what Dr. Elmore's math "Ah! Hah!" moment discussed above is about.

This was also the impetus for us to structure this book a bit differently than we had originally planned to do. Rather than schools focusing so heavily on learning itself, which is counterproductive since students naturally rebel at anything adults are forcing them to do, why not focus on the things that students tend to do naturally? What about using their natural desire to explore their world as the basis for their school experience? If we can create school as a set of rich experiences for students,

Figure I-7: *True engagement is about living, playing and creating. Early Childhood Center at Shorecrest Prep School in St. Petersburg, Florida.*

then we will, by extension, also be providing rich opportunities for learning.

We wanted to parallel these experiences with a student's life outside school and find the equivalent experiences during the school day and focus on those. The book's structure was derived from this line of thinking, and so we have our major sections as Live, Play, Engage, and Create. All the learning that students need to function as successful adults can be obtained as they alternate between these four states of being and doing.

> If we can create school as a set of rich experiences for students, then we will, by extension, also be providing rich opportunities for learning.

Live, Play, Engage, and Create are Integrated

For clarity, we have looked separately at the four elements of Live, Play, Engage, and Create. However, we want to stress that these are not ironclad distinctions but parts of an integrated whole. Depending on the context in which they are analyzed, each of the four elements may have smaller or greater aspects of the other elements within them. That means a student who is obviously "playing" could also be "living," "engaging," and "creating."

Keeping this important qualifier in mind, let us look briefly at what will be covered under these four sections as described in the book:

Live

"Live" covers all the aspects of the school experience that has to do with students in their individual and social milieu at school. It is also the realm that provides the greatest opportunities for emotional and spiritual growth and nourishment. Here are the areas we cover under the "live" category:

- Group collaboration
- Relaxing
- Meditating
- Physical fitness
- Socializing
- Eating
- Taking care of animals
- Gardening
- Community service

Play

By some measures, play is quickly becoming the dominant form of learning in this century. From a very early age, children use play as a simulation of life itself. Think about these characteristics of spontaneous play – this list applies as much to a game of chess as it does to soccer. It is natural; it

> Most of what is taught in classroom settings is forgotten, and much or what is remembered is irrelevant.
> — *Ben Johnson*

is dynamic; it is creative; it requires strategy; it helps you learn from mistakes; and it is engaging and exciting. This list is the very essence of what we would want the whole school experience to be. Here are the areas that we cover in the "play" category:

- Social games
- Games with manipulatives
- Physical activity play/sports
- Creative play with different materials
- Computer games
- Playing in nature

> Students need to be fully "engaged" for the real value of their learning to be realized.

Engage

"Engage" is about the more familiar things we normally associate with school, primarily in the area of academic growth and achievement. Ironically, by focusing so heavily on academics, schools often lose the opportunity to showcase such learning not as an end unto itself, but in service of some higher purpose. The hard and, sometimes, uninspiring work students need to do in this realm can only be fully rationalized for its long-term value when students can see direct connections between theory and practice and understand why the academic aspects of school will benefit them at a very personal level. In other words, students need to be fully "engaged" for the real value of their learning to be realized. Such engagement has to go beyond the desire to please a teacher or do well on an exam. Let us keep referring back to Prof. Elmore's definition of learning which requires students to "consciously" engage with an activity as a prelude to "modifying" their worldview and "learning" something. Here are the areas covered in this book under the "Engage" category:

- Direct Instruction
- Reading
- Research
- Experimentation
- Cooperative Learning
- Entrepreneurship
- Presentations
- Internships
- Projects

Create

"Create" is what schools for today and tomorrow are about. Just pause for a moment and contemplate the billions of pages of information, games, music, services, courses, and specific tools for skill-building that are available online. Now ask yourself how much of this vast treasure trove of resources is consumed rather than produced by students while they are

> Just pause for a moment and contemplate the billions of pages of information, games, music, services, courses, and specific tools for skill-building that are available online.

INTRODUCTION BACK TO THE FUTURE

Figure I-8: *The best learning happens when teachers become mentors, coaches and role models. The obsession with "teaching" is actually the most significant roadblock to real learning.*

in schools. It is a safe bet that while youth around the world are prolific in the extent to which they make creative contributions to the resources on the Internet, it is an equally safe bet that the vast majority of these contributions don't happen while they are in school. When students go from being passive consumers to active contributors to the Internet, not only will the world benefit from the vast untapped potential that is locked away in our young people, but we are also able to better prepare them for the creative and challenging lives and careers they can successfully navigate and thrive in. We cover these areas under the "create" category:

- Music
- Performance
- Fine Arts
- Cooking and baking
- Technology-assisted media

> True learning requires both theory and practice — knowing and doing.

- Writing
- Making and building things

Foundational Beliefs of this Book

1. **Schools are places for learning, not teaching:** Oscar Wilde may have been onto something when he said, "Education is an admirable thing, but it is well to remember from time to time that nothing that is worth learning can be taught." Unfortunately, what students experience in schools is a lot of teaching and not enough learning. Schools thus become places where children go to watch adults work. "Traditional education incorrectly assumes that for every ounce of teaching there is an ounce of learning by those who are taught. However, most of what we learn before, during, and after attending schools is learned without its being taught to us. A child learns such fundamental things as how to walk, talk, eat, dress, and so on without being taught these things. Adults learn most of what they use at work or at leisure while at work or leisure. Most of what is taught in classroom settings is forgotten, and much of what is remembered is irrelevant."[2] So what does a teacher do and why do we need them in schools? "Great teachers engineer learning experiences that maneuver the students into the driver's seat and then the teachers get out of the way."[3] Teachers can be many things that inspire students to learn. They can be coaches, they can be counselors and they can be role models for great learning. What they shouldn't be is obsessed with teaching as a way to impart learning.

2. **Education should be about learning, not just knowing:** While knowing is embedded in real learning, it is entirely possible to "know" something without having "learned" it. We can "know" all there is to know about how to drive a car from textbooks and videos but we don't truly "learn" how to drive a car until we sit behind the wheel. Thus true learning requires both theory and practice — knowing and doing. However, much of what schools do is about ensuring that students "know" the material in the curriculum regardless of whether they have truly "learned" it or not.

3. De-emphasize the obsession in school with "preparing" for the future: Everything about the education system from the days of early childhood education through graduating from high school, college, graduate school, and beyond is about preparing for what comes next. Nursery school kids are told how important it is to "prepare" for kindergarten and kindergartners are told to prepare for the 1st grade and so on. This unending series of milestones that are just ahead and out of reach that children are trained to pursue comes at a heavy cost. It prioritizes a vague and illusory future over the real and tangible present.

   According to Alan Watts, "If happiness always depends on something expected in the future, we are chasing a will-o'-the-wisp that ever eludes our grasp, until the future, and ourselves vanish into the abyss of death."[4]

---

[2] The Objective of Education Is Learning, Not Teaching. Public Policy. Knowledge@Wharton. University of Pennsylvania. http://knowledge.wharton.upenn.edu/article/the-objective-of-education-is-learning-not-teaching/
[3] Great Teachers Don't Teach by Ben Johnson, Edutopia, June 28, 2013. https://www.edutopia.org/blog/great-teachers-do-not-teach-ben-johnson
[4] Alan Watts: 'Why modern education is a hoax' by Mike Colagrossi, 25 September, 2018. Big Think. https://bigthink.com/personal-growth/alan-watts-education

INTRODUCTION BACK TO THE FUTURE

"Now rather than falling into a passive nihilism (which is where Buddhist thought can lead) Alan Watts instead argues for being within the here and now. Learn for learning's sake! Eternity is now... that is to become fully part of the process—whatever it may be—and do not focus on an ever elusive end goal."[5]

> **Rich learning experiences occur at the nexus of great environments and a compelling curriculum.**

How this Book Came About

When this book began as a germ of an idea in early 2017, the two original authors were at very different stages in their professional careers. One (Prakash) had more than 18 years' experience working on the design of innovative schools worldwide and the other (Roni) had just begun her journey with only a couple of years as an innovative schools designer. Our third key author, Prof. Richard Elmore, had initially agreed to write a chapter on learning and design to give greater clarity to these elements but what he ended up producing felt, to us, to be more than a chapter, which is why we decided to carve out an entire section of the book dedicated to his thoughts on the subject.

What all of us have in common is our passion to keep pushing against the education establishment – and anyone else who will

Rich learning experiences occur at the nexus of great environments and a compelling curriculum

Figure I-9: *What we call "learning" involves what and how it is learned (the formal or informal "curriculum") as well as the "where" it is learned (the learning environment). The holistic experience that we can call learning is actually at the nexus of the curriculum and the environment. That means, truly rich learning experiences happen at the nexus of a great environment and a compelling curriculum.*

---

[5] Ibid

listen, for that matter — to bring about a new and better way to educate children. This is an imperative that grows more urgent with each passing year with the momentous changes the world itself is experiencing. Our common passion for education became the foundation for this writing partnership.

The vastly different perspectives we brought to this project given our vastly different life and career paths have allowed us to present a broader view of the subject than any one of us might have been able to on our own. Most of the collaborative work on this book happened remotely and via video conferences. However, the times that we were able to work side-by-side and, particularly, the times we were able to visit the schools featured in this book to meet and talk directly to teachers and students, brought forth the best ideas and, represent for us, the most inspiring and satisfying aspects of writing this book.

This book has been an amazing journey of discovery for us and we hope it will be for you as well. Every school we visited, every educator we met with and each student we talked to taught us something new. We had believed we would first need to tear down the education establishment so that a new one could be built in its place. Now, we realize that is not absolutely necessary. Instead, we have chosen to show how schooling and education as we have known it are dead but that learning is alive and well. What role schools should play to remain relevant in the years ahead is the question this book seeks to answer. What we are certain about is this: Rich learning experiences occur at the nexus of great environments and a compelling curriculum.

CHAPTER 1
THE EDUCATIONAL UNDERPINNING FOR GOOD SPACE DESIGN

Why do school facilities need to change? After all, one could argue, the current model of school has worked well for well over a hundred years. Over this time, many educational models have come and gone and, yet, the traditional school building design has soldiered on. So why change? Well, here is the most obvious reason:

The Purpose of Education has Changed: Education used to be about instilling "knowledge" into students, which is a fancy way of saying that education's primary purpose was to "teach" students "stuff." In the traditional educational model, the more "knowledge" one had, the more educated he or she was. But one doesn't need to go to school anymore for knowledge. There is a growing stock of information and tutorials of all kinds ready at hand on the Internet so that we are all free to learn anything, anytime, anywhere. With knowledge becoming an easily available commodity, education must now be about building strong

Figure 1-1: *Task Predicts Performance. Students get good at what they do. At this senior student center at Centaurus High School in Boulder Valley, Colorado, students get to spend time with their peers or working independently to complete tasks at their own pace.*

1 CHAPTER THE EDUCATIONAL UNDERPINNING FOR GOOD SPACE DESIGN

social, creative, and conceptual thinking skills, building character and a whole range of new literacies. According to the World Economic Forum's "Future of Jobs" report, the top 10 job skills for 2020 will be[6]:

1. Complex problem solving
2. Critical thinking
3. Creativity
4. People management
5. Coordinating with others
6. Emotional intelligence
7. Judgment and decision-making
8. Service orientation
9. Negotiation
10. Cognitive flexibility

> With knowledge becoming an easily available commodity, education must now be about building strong social, creative, and conceptual thinking skills.

Dr. Richard Elmore has an elegant saying, "Task Predicts Performance." That means, students need to be doing things in school that we want them to be good at as adults. Since we know what the top job skills for the future are, shouldn't we be designing student experiences in school that allow them to practice and perfect these skills? Clearly, the traditional classroom limited by its physical design and further encumbered by a teacher-directed pedagogy, offers little opportunity for students to practice and perfect the above list of ten future skills.

Four Key Domains of the Educational System

Let us look at four distinct domains of the educational "system". There is near-consensus among school reformers that each of these four domains needs a radical shift in order to best serve the new educational model represented by the new literacies noted above. Taken together, the shift in all four domains represents a whole new paradigm of education. What we are talking about is the "software" of education and how it has changed radically and irrevocably over the past couple of decades since the dawn of the Internet era.

It follows that the "hardware" of education — in particular the buildings in which education is conducted — must also change to "run" the new "software." We will discuss the nature of the shift in each domain, and demonstrate why the traditional "cells and bells" (factory model with classrooms and corridors) school design is unsuited to accommodate the changes. From there, we will present a new "learning community" model that can become a template not only for the design of new schools but also for the renovation of existing school buildings.

Shifts in the Four Domains of Education

Teacher Practice — From Solo to Collaborative Teams: The "classroom teacher" is a staple of education systems worldwide. One might even say it is the bedrock foundation of everything we know

> "Task Predicts Performance." That means, students need to be doing things in school that we want them to be good at as adults.

---

[6] The 10 skills you need to thrive in the Fourth Industrial Revolution by Alex Grey. World Economic Forum
https://www.weforum.org/agenda/2016/01/the-10-skills-you-need-to-thrive-in-the-fourth-industrial-revolution/

1 CHAPTER THE EDUCATIONAL UNDERPINNING FOR GOOD SPACE DESIGN

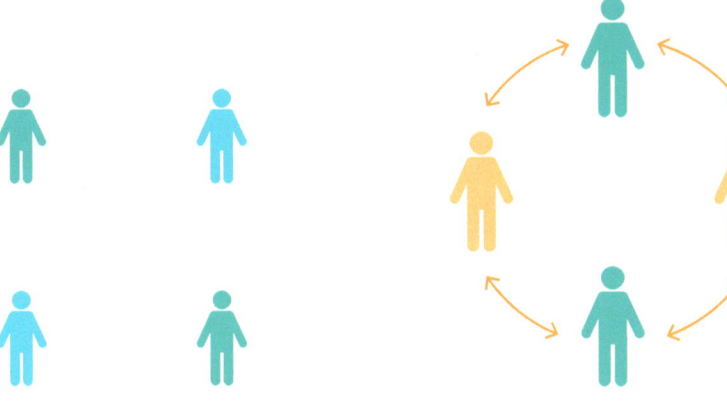

Teachers work independently, isolated in classrooms

Teachers work as part of a team in a learning community

Figure 1-2: *When teachers are trapped in individual classrooms, they are perpetually in a fixed teacher – student ratio. This makes it nearly impossible to personalize or differentiate learning. When teachers work as a team, they can personalize learning. In this model, working one-on-one with a student or a small group will be possible since the remaining students can be supervised by the rest of the teaching team.*

as school; a single adult at the front of a room full of students sorted by age and grade. Teaching in school has largely been a solo practice and, to this day, remains the predominant way in which teachers work. Teachers being trapped alone with a bunch of students in a room for most of the school day is an undeniable and inescapable function of the way in which schools are designed with classrooms as their basic building block.

There is a strong educational rationale to change this model so that teachers have more opportunities — ideally throughout the school day — to work as part of a team. The research is clear on this. When teachers collaborate, student achievement improves. A Stanford study makes the compelling argument that when it comes to teachers, "social capital," which is measured by teachers' ability to interact frequently with their peers, has far greater value as measured by student achievement than "human

Figure 1-3: *Teachers work collaboratively as a team in their professional office and get to interact with each other regularly throughout the school day. This is a big change from the model where teachers own classrooms which are also their de-facto offices. Isolation in teacher-owned classrooms comes at a steep price because it sharply curtails the opportunity to collaborate and work as a team. Hillel School, Tampa, Florida.*

1 CHAPTER THE EDUCATIONAL UNDERPINNING FOR GOOD SPACE DESIGN

Figure 1-4: *Classrooms send a powerful message to students that they are there to listen to and take direction from the teacher. Common and breakout areas provide the ideal environments in which teachers can step aside and let students direct their own learning.*

capital," which represents the professional development classes and certifications that teachers receive.[7] The value of professional collaboration is further enhanced when teachers are afforded sufficient time during the school day to keep up with the latest research and developments in their own fields of expertise.

Pedagogy — From Teacher-Directed to Student-Directed: The classroom is perfectly designed to have one adult direct the work of several students under his or her charge. Consider the manner in which most classrooms are laid out. There is usually a desk for the teacher in front of the room and the rest of the room is filled with student desks and chairs. There is a "teaching wall" that contains a whiteboard and (sometimes) an electronic smart board. Very often the student desks and chairs are lined up to face the front of the room. Classrooms send a powerful message to students that they are there to listen to and take direction from the teacher. Even when teachers want to change the model to empower students by joining tables to create collaborative student groupings, the fundamental structure of the room remains one of control where one adult is fully in charge of what happens, how it happens and where it happens.

The teacher-centered model of education is now outdated because the kinds of skills it is best designed to develop such as rote learning, content mastery, memorization, and academic fluency are quickly giving way to the 21st century literacies noted at the start of this chapter. Beyond the need to change the educational model so as to make it more relevant to today's world, we also have to consider the question of student agency and autonomy. Prof. Elmore talks about this in Part Two of this book when he refers to the four "theories of learning" that determine how we set up schools.

The research is clear on this. When teachers collaborate, student achievement improves.

---

[7] *The Missing Link in School Reform*, Carrie R. Leanna, Stanford Social Innovation Review 2011
https://www2.ed.gov/programs/slcp/2011progdirmtg/mislinkinrfm.pdf

Figure 1-5: *This space that used to be a teacher-directed computer lab has been reconfigured so that it encourages teachers to step aside and let students manage their own time and direct their own learning.*
Middle School iLab at the Academy of the Holy Names in Tampa, Florida.

Hierarchical models, no matter how earnestly they wish to promote a student's best interests, have an intrinsic problem in that students don't like to be told what to do! There is also the practical reality that students will "learn" better — meaning they will get good at developing important and relevant skills needed for success in college, career and life — when they are actually practicing those skills while they are in school. Classrooms are simply not optimized to accommodate the wide range of activities associated with the new 21st century literacies. The imperatives for why it is critical to change from a teacher-directed to a student-directed model of education is discussed in greater detail in *Blueprint for Tomorrow — Redesigning Spaces for Student Centered Learning.*[8]

Curriculum — From Segregated Subjects to Interdisciplinary Courses: Most classrooms have labels on them announcing the name of the teacher who lives there and the subject he or she teaches. And so we have a math classroom, a science classroom (and lab), an English classroom, a social studies classroom and maybe even a computer classroom. The arrangement of a school into a series of classrooms leads naturally into this model of labeling the rooms and assigning them to an adult who specializes

> " Classrooms send a powerful message to students that they are there to listen to and take direction from the teacher.

---

[8] *Blueprint for Tomorrow, Redesigning Schools for Student Centered Learning* by Prakash Nair. Harvard Education Press, 2014

1 CHAPTER THE EDUCATIONAL UNDERPINNING FOR GOOD SPACE DESIGN

Figure 1-6: *This commons space is part of a learning community that connects several learning studios. It serves as an ideal environment to encourage teachers to collaborate so that they can design and deliver an interdisciplinary curriculum. Middle School learning community at the Academy of the Holy Names in Tampa, Florida.*

in teaching one subject. Of course, in the early grades, homeroom teachers may teach more than one subject but, even here, the school day is broken down into periods devoted to the teaching of individual subjects like math and English.

There is no scientific rationale for the way the school building and the school day are broken down into bite-sized chunks of space called classrooms and bite-sized chunks of time called periods. In other words, we have no evidence that this is a good way to teach or learn anything. What we do know is that this kind of education militates against our stated goal of preparing students with the skills and competencies they need for college, career, and life. In the words of David Orr, "A fourth myth of higher education is that we can adequately restore that which we have dismantled. In the modern curriculum we have fragmented the world into bits and pieces called disciplines and subdisciplines. As a result, after 12 or 16 or 20 years of education, most students graduate without any broad integrated sense of

Beyond the need to change the educational model so as to make it more relevant to today's world, we also have to consider the question of student agency and autonomy.

Figure 1-7: *The advantage of breaking away from the classroom-based model of school design in favor of the learning community model is that students will have more opportunities to learn and socialize with a larger group of their peers – often across grade levels. Kevin Bartlett High School, International School of Brussels, Belgium.*

the unity of things."[9]

Interdisciplinary courses are needed for students to have opportunities to see that disciplines are not self-contained fragments of information and knowledge, but parts of a larger whole. Heidi Hayes Jacobs says, "In the real world, we do not wake up in the morning and do social studies for 50 minutes. The adolescent begins to realize that in real life we encounter problems and situations, gather data from all of our resources, and generate solutions. The fragmented school day does not reflect this reality." [10]

It is true that in a field like medicine, specialization and super-specialization has been common in the past but,

> Classrooms are simply not optimized to accommodate the wide range of activities associated with the new 21st century literacies.

---

[9] What Is Education For? Six myths about the foundations of modern education, and six new principles to replace them By David Orr. One of the articles in The Learning Revolution (IC#27) Originally published in Winter 1991 on page 52

[10] Interdisciplinary Curriculum, The Growing Need for Interdisciplinary Curriculum Content by Heidi Hayes Jacobs. Edited for ASCD by Heidi Hayes Jacobs from her book, Interdisciplinary Curriculum, Design and Implementation, ASCD, 1989. Published online at: http://www.ascd.org/publications/books/61189156/chapters/The-Growing-Need-for-Interdisciplinary-Curriculum-Content.aspx

today, doctors are also being asked to see their practice within the larger context of the human body, which is a complex, interdependent system driven not only by its biology but also by more abstract aspects such as mind and spirit.

It is beyond the scope of this book to discuss the details of how interdisciplinary curriculums work except that they can only work when two or more teachers design and are able to implement the interdisciplinary unit together. Interdisciplinary curriculum units also tend to provide a greater opportunity to design student experiences that fit the Live:Play:Engage:Create paradigm around which we argue that schools must be designed. Such curriculums also provide students the greatest opportunity to bring their own natural skills and personal experiences to bear on the problems they confront in school and, as a result, make education more democratic and less autocratic.

> A new "learning community" model can become a template not only for the design of new schools but also for the renovation of existing school buildings.

Community — From Classroom to Network: As knowledge and information become commodities, the purpose of school becomes less about formal content learning and more about social and emotional development and about giving students opportunities to participate in and function as effective members of a close-knit community. In traditional schools, and particularly in large public schools, the classroom cohort has tended to serve as a student's primary school "community." Given the constraints of the space design and the rigidity of school schedules, students rarely have time to build real friendships with others outside their classroom or develop close connections with other caring teachers with whom they spend scant time — usually in the company of 20 or 30 other students. From a learning perspective, the lack of a community that extends beyond the classroom is an even bigger concern in today's world. Today, more than ever before, students need to be able to meet and mingle with larger, more diverse groups than would be available within an age-restricted classroom cohort. Similarly, students need to be able to work and consult with several adults who bring different perspectives and worldviews to enrich learning.

The Network model is about a more democratic, and less hierarchical, organization of learning spaces and people. This model does not do well within the constraints of a traditional classroom, which is the ultimate representation of hierarchy and control.

Connecting the Hardware and Software of Education

Almost every school has seven key organizational components or "teaching and learning practices" in play that, taken together, will provide the most accurate picture of that particular school's "Theory of Learning," which is described in detail in Part Two of this book. While the organizational components themselves are common to all schools, they are, each of them, implementable according to a spectrum. On the left-hand side of the spectrum are practices that represent a more traditional teaching and learning model, and on the right-hand side are practices that are becoming more prevalent as schools work hard to better prepare students with the skills they need for today and tomorrow. That is not to say that the right side of the spectrum is "good" and the left is "bad." It is more a matter of picking the side that best suits the learning needs of students at any moment in time. That means, ideally, schools need to be set up in a way that allows for free movement across each spectrum.

> The Network model is about a more democratic, and less hierarchical, organization of learning spaces and people.

1 CHAPTER THE EDUCATIONAL UNDERPINNING FOR GOOD SPACE DESIGN

From a "software" standpoint, we have established that the school user community have an organizational need to move freely from the left side of each component to the right and back to the left side when and as needed. With this in mind, let us look at the "hardware" of schools represented by the school building to see how well it supports the free movement of each organizational component across all seven components.

The red line that is drawn vertically across all seven spectrums represents the manner in which an antiquated cells and bells school building will, literally and physically, prevent free movement from the left side of each component to the right. To illustrate, let us look at the first component, which is teacher collaboration. This is the situation in which individual teachers

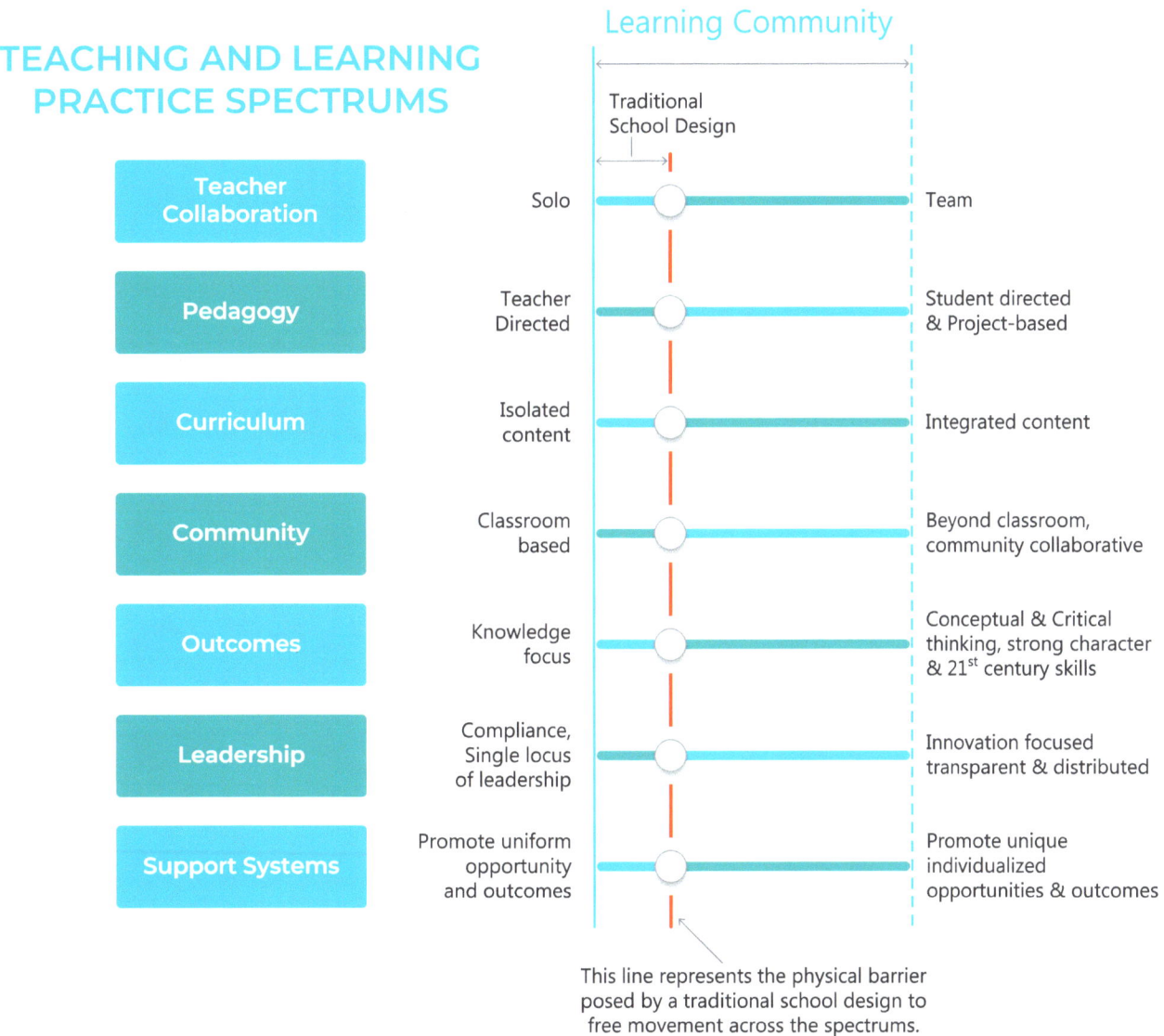

Figure 1-8: *The red line that is drawn vertically across all the seven spectrums represents the manner in which an antiquated cells and bells school building will, literally and physically, prevent free movement from the left side of each component to the right. This provides a compelling argument for why the physical design of school needs to be changed so that the building does not stand in the way of schools that choose to move from the Hierarchical model of education to the Distributed model (discussed in Part Two of this book).*

1 CHAPTER THE EDUCATIONAL UNDERPINNING FOR GOOD SPACE DESIGN

teach in individual classrooms. This model directly and overtly "prefers" the solo teaching model at the left-hand side of the spectrum and militates against teachers working together as a team.

In the same way, the cells and bells school building favors a teacher-directed pedagogy and militates against a student-directed model simply because classrooms are optimized for teacher direction, control, and lecture and has severe limitations when it comes to things like peer tutoring, team collaboration, independent study, research, and so on.

INDIVIDUALLY OWNED ROOMS

Optimized for: Individualized teaching practices, traditional structures and timetable, classroom - based community, single teacher classrooms, teacher - directed learning

SHARED IN A PAIR

Optimized for: Pairings within grade, department and/ or interdisciplinary, shared unit/lesson design, co - delivery, flexible/dynamic groupings, more varied learning modalities, shared assessment, easier for project - based, more options for breakout

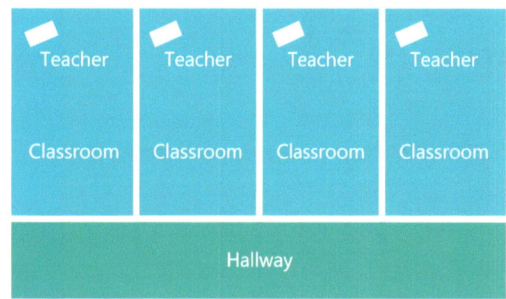

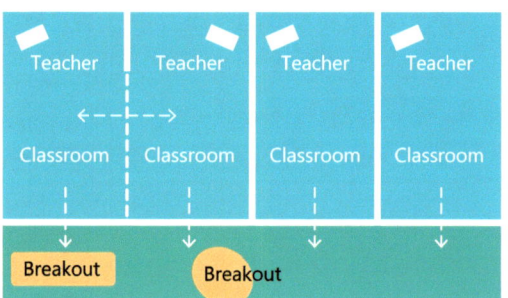

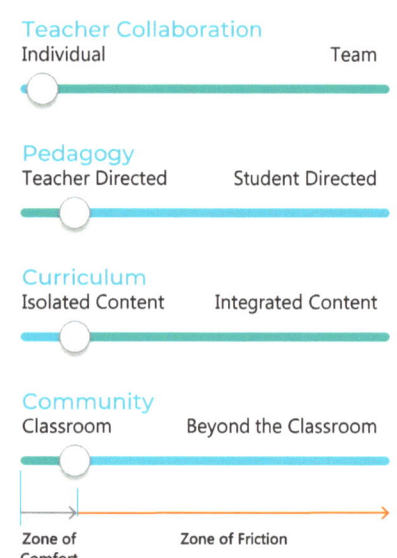

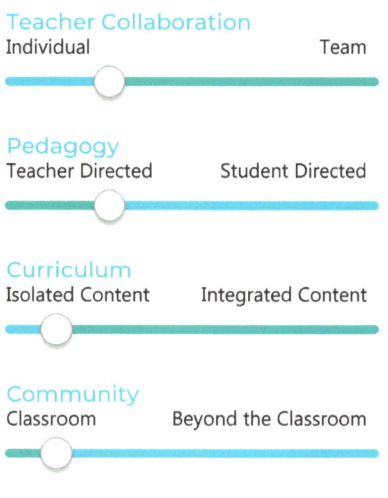

Figure 1-9: *These diagrams show how the "hardware" of schools – the learning spaces – have a direct and profound impact on the "software" of education represented by teacher collaboration, pedagogy, curriculum and community. Even minor changes in the way schools are designed can substantially impact teaching and learning.*

This line of reasoning can be applied across all seven components, but it is useful to look at the last one, which is "support systems." In our assessment, a cells and bells school is designed to promote uniform opportunity and outcome for all students because classrooms are, basically, about groups and not about individuals. In the classroom model, it has become prohibitively difficult to create a model where each student is offered unique, individualized opportunities to learn and grow.

> The cells and bells school building favors a teacher-directed pedagogy and militates against a student-directed model.

It is obvious from this discussion that the "hardware" represented by antiquated buildings places severe constraints on a school's ability to move from a "Hierarchical" to a "Distributed" model of education — discussed in Part Two of this book. The way out of this dilemma is to create a physical design of school in which the black line would completely disappear. That means, the architecture will facilitate free movement across all seven organizational components.

In the series of graphics shown below, we have illustrated the direct connections between what we call the educational "software" and the "hardware" on which it "runs," represented by the physical learning environment. We have narrowed the list of organizational components to just four domains for convenience, although the diagrams would be just as applicable if all seven were represented.

The first diagram, titled "Individually Owned Classrooms," shows how the traditional design of schools with individual teacher-owned classrooms keeps all four domains discussed in this chapter squarely at the left end of the spectrum. This demonstrates how the existing hardware represented by traditional school buildings is simply incapable of running the essential software of today's education.

In the second diagram, titled "Shared in a Pair," we show how even a modest change to the physical space, represented by the opening up of walls between pairs of classrooms, begins to move each bar within the four domains towards the right end of the spectrum. That is because 1) teachers can now work as a team; 2) with two adults supervising, more modes of student-centered learning can be introduced; 3) teachers are able to jointly design and deliver an interdisciplinary curriculum; and 4) students are now members of a community that extends beyond the limits of their own classroom. Personalization now becomes more possible. This is the kind of physical change that even cash-strapped schools and school districts can afford, and the changes can easily be completed during the summer break.

The third diagram, titled "The Learning Community," is optimized for the educational software bars to move freely along the full length of the spectrum within each domain. This is a representational diagram and not intended to be seen as a prototypical design. Actual learning community designs vary widely and can be adapted to a variety of traditional building types. Naturally, new schools can also be designed

> The learning community offers a lot of benefits in that it is an agile, dynamic space that can quickly adapt to changes in population, pedagogy, and curriculum. Learning Communities are about building strong social, creative, and conceptual thinking skills.

around the idea of learning communities. In our experience, traditional cells and bells schools can be reconfigured as learning communities without a huge investment of capital dollars and, almost always, such changes can be accomplished over the summer break.

From an operational standpoint also, the learning community offers a lot of benefits in that it is an agile, dynamic space that can quickly adapt to changes in population, pedagogy, and curriculum. It is the quintessential representation of a "Learning Building"[11] — a building that evolves over time as it "learns" from the users who occupy the space.

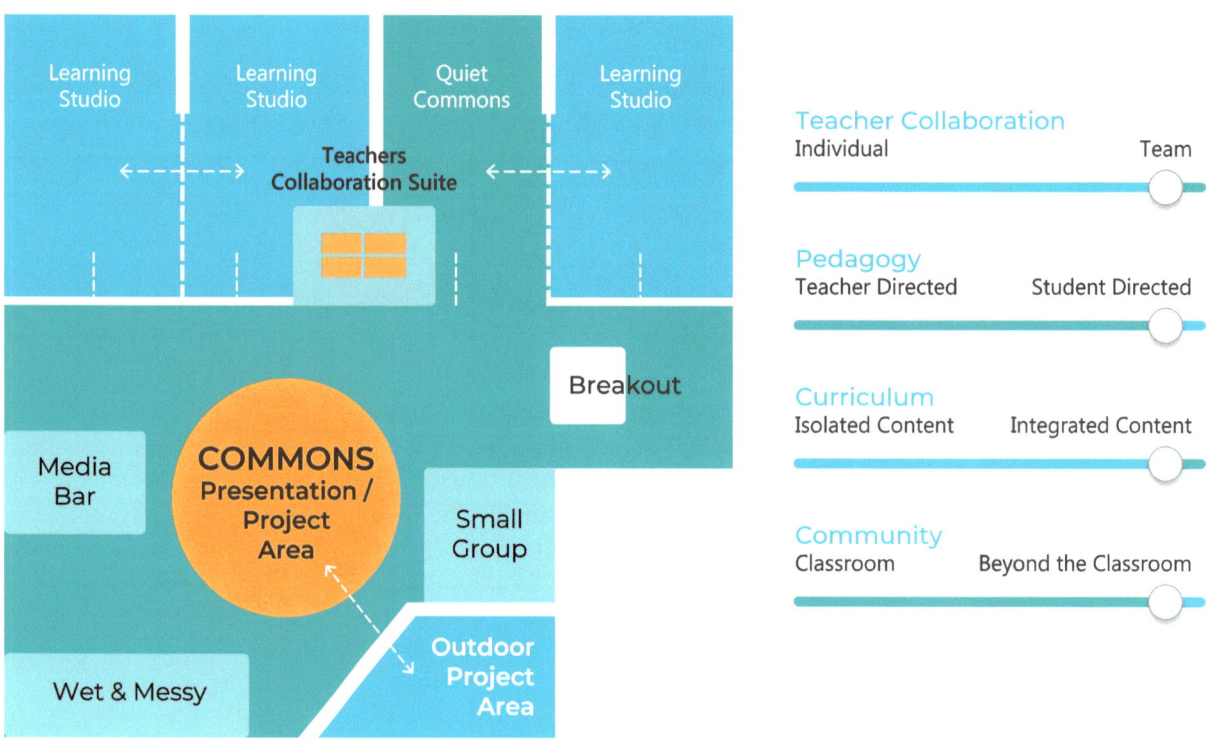

Figure 1-10: *The hardware-software connection comes into full force in this model of space design where there are no individually owned classrooms. There are a wide variety of spaces to facilitate different modalities of learning and a much richer curriculum than would be permitted under the traditional cells-and-bells model of classrooms aligned along a corridor.*

---

[11] Blueprint for Tomorrow, Redesigning Schools for Student Centered Learning by Prakash Nair, Harvard Education Press, 2014

CHAPTER 2
EIGHT PRINCIPLES THAT DEFINE THE NEW SCHOOL DESIGN PARADIGM

Authentic

That learning experiences should be authentic should not even be up for debate — what other kind of learning is there? Our answer to that, unfortunately, would be schooling itself. Schooling is designed to formalize learning so that adults can measure students' "progress" along predetermined paths they have set down. This formal process sacrifices authenticity for simplicity and, in doing so, militates against the very thing schools are supposed to do — encourage students to "learn" as a means toward realizing their own unique, individual potential.

So what is authentic learning and how does this look different from the hierarchically directed "formal" learning that predominates the student experience in schools? A simple way to describe "authentic" is to look at a school's sports team. In this instance, the work students do to become better as individuals and as a team is abundantly clear. There is a direct cause and effect relationship between their efforts and the results they see on the field. There is also the reality they must face of their own limitations and to what

extent these can be overcome with hard work, teamwork, and coaching.

With sports, the results of the work students do can also be measured by real outcomes. This alignment between student achievement and adults' need to measure success allows sports to function as one of very few truly authentic experiences that students experience in schools. There is also an important component of self-selection that is part and parcel of the "authenticity" that is found in sports. Students who participate in sports are there because they

> **"** Authentic learning is about students' exposure to subjects in a manner that resembles what professionals in the field do on a daily basis.

Figure 2-1, 2-2: *The theoretical work done in the school attains greater meaning when it is based on real-world experiences. Hiking in nature is as authentic as it gets. There are numerous opportunities for students of all ages to acquire a variety of useful skills on a nature walk such as teamwork, observation, endurance, and learning about the natural world that is far removed from the screens on their digital gadgets.*

want to be and because they see themselves as playing the real game the professionals play — even when they know they aren't as good as those at the top of the game.

Success measures in sports can go beyond winning or losing. Students can be rewarded for their efforts, for the real progress they make as a result of the work they do and the extent to which they support their team to succeed. Sports also contain many non-measurable benefits like discipline, persistence, teamwork, self-confidence, and learning how to deal with and overcome failure.

Go into the classroom now and look at the way mathematics is taught and "learned" in schools. First, how many are there because they want to be mathematicians? Second, how does what happens in a math classroom compare to what professional mathematicians do? There is a superb essay on this subject called "The Mathematician's Lament" by Paul Lockhart.[12] It illustrates why what math students are forced to do in school bears almost no resemblance to the real world of mathematics. The overwhelming majority of students who study math in schools will do so without

---

[12] A Mathematician's Lament by Paul Lockhart. https://www.maa.org/external_archive/devlin/LockhartsLament.pdf

2 CHAPTER EIGHT PRINCIPLES THAT DEFINE THE NEW SCHOOL DESIGN PARADIGM

THE 20 MODALITIES OF LEARNING

1. Independent Study
2. Peer-to-peer Tutoring
3. One-on-one with Teacher
4. Lecture
5. Team Collaboration
6. Project-based Learning
7. Distance Learning
8. Learning with Mobile Technology
9. Student Presentation
10. Internet-based Research
11. Seminar-style Instruction
12. Performance-based Learning
13. Interdisciplinary Study
14. Naturalist Learning
15. Art-based Learning
16. Social-Emotional Learning
17. Design-based Learning
18. Storytelling
19. Team Learning and Teaching
20. Play and Movement Learning

being exposed to the real beauty of the subject.

Making math learning "authentic" will require a radical retooling not only of the curriculum but also the way it is learned in schools. Children can exist at various points in the spectrum of becoming professional mathematicians — most will, of course, not go on to become professionals just as most students will not play professional sports — but wherever they are, they will be there by choice and because they see the utility of math in their own lives.

This discussion about mathematics is equally true of all the other subjects like English, social studies, science and languages. Authentic learning is about students' exposure to these subjects in a manner that resembles what professionals in the field do on a daily basis and not the watered-down one-size-fits-all simulations that students experience in schools.

Figures 2-3: *Schools can only truly transform when they understand that it is OK for students, even when they are in the same space, to be doing different things. Unlike a traditional classroom in which every student has a similar desk and chair, a well-designed space for learning will provide a variety of seating and working options that students will naturally select and gravitate toward based on what they are learning and who they are learning with.*

2 CHAPTER EIGHT PRINCIPLES THAT DEFINE THE NEW SCHOOL DESIGN PARADIGM

Figure 2-4: *In a common area like this, which is an essential part of a learning community, far more modalities of learning will be possible than in the learning studios which are more suitable for group instruction. Look at this image from the perspective of the 20 modalities of learning and it will become immediately apparent that it will accommodate almost all of them. Such spaces are "dynamic" and "living" in the sense that they can be easily configured and reconfigured to serve teaching and learning.*
Kevin Bartlett High School at the International School of Brussels.

Multi-Modal

The way classrooms are designed leaves little room for modes of learning beyond the artificial teacher-directed exercises that students are forced to do. Classrooms themselves, the places where students spend most of their school day, are severely limited when it comes to the modalities of learning they will comfortably accommodate. Look at the 20 modalities of learning listed above and transpose them into a classroom setting. How many can a traditional classroom accommodate well? Two or three maybe? Classrooms are well designed for teacher and student presentations but fall short when measured by their ability to deliver the other modes of learning.

By multi-modal, we are saying that students need to select the mode of learning that is best aligned with two criteria: 1) what they are learning and 2) how they would like to learn it. What is being learned is only one piece of the puzzle. It does not tell us how any particular student may choose to learn it. Just as some students are happy to learn in the hustle and bustle of a Starbucks while others prefer a quiet corner somewhere, so also students in school need choices so that they have the opportunity to become comfortable in

> Classrooms are well designed for teacher and student presentations but fall short when measured by their ability to deliver the other modes of learning.

their environment as a prelude to learning whatever it is they are learning.

Interdisciplinary

There is beauty in the purity of each subject and we appreciate why there are instances where it is important to see a subject in its own special light. Subjects in school are not there because of this high ideal of presenting their beauty and purity to students. They are there because of the ease with which this kind of artificial way to segment learning allows the school day to be broken up into bite-sized chunks of time.

We challenge schools to expose students to the interdisciplinary nature of everything they will encounter in their lives. It is hardly a secret that we are now in a changing world where almost every desirable job has interdisciplinary elements. This trend is not just here to stay but accelerating at a pace that makes it impossible to ignore. Schools have begun to take notice and efforts to make the

Figures 2-5, 2-6: *Almost everything in life is interdisciplinary and schools should be no exception. Students are much more likely to be engaged in their work when they can see the connections between disciplines. This can be done via projects in Maker Rooms or STEAM labs that let them apply math, science and engineering concepts in a creative way.*
Maker Lab at Hillel School of Detroit, Michigan.

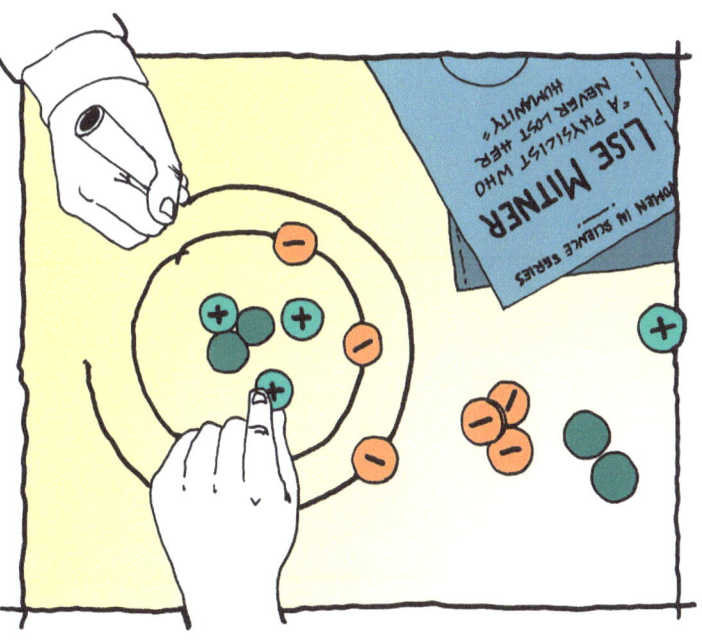

2 CHAPTER EIGHT PRINCIPLES THAT DEFINE THE NEW SCHOOL DESIGN PARADIGM

Figure 2-7: *No matter what modality of learning is used, and no matter if it is happening alone, with a teacher or with peers, all learning is, ultimately, personal. Every student constructs learning based on his or her own life experiences and predispositions. Understanding this very fundamental rule about learning is the first step toward moving away from the mass-production model of schooling and toward a personalized model in which each student is seen as a completely unique person with completely unique aptitudes and interests. One-on-one learning with a teacher at American School of Bombay, Mumbai.*

student experiences more interdisciplinary can be found in project-based offerings, STEAM curriculums, service learning, and internship opportunities. These programs stand out for the manner in which they engage students to become more active participants in their own learning. Despite their obvious benefits, schools are reluctant to dive in with both feet and become more interdisciplinary. This reluctance comes from their efforts to juggle two basically incompatible paradigms – the old teacher-directed, classroom-based, subject-driven educational model against the new student-directed, experience-based, interdisciplinary model. Real change from the old, familiar but completely obsolete educational model can only happen when we replace not just parts of the old model, but introduce a whole new one. Please refer to the chapter in this book on Pathfinder Projects that illustrates one effective way to introduce real, meaningful, holistic, and sustainable change.

Personal

We have chosen to use the term "Personal" and not "Personalized." These two terms are derived from the same understanding that no two students are exactly alike. They recognize that education needs to move away from the one-size-fits-all model to a model where individual differences are recognized and celebrated. But let us look at each term

> We challenge schools to expose students to the interdisciplinary nature of everything they will encounter in their lives.

to understand why we prefer to use the term "Personal."

Personalized education assumes that an adult, like a tailor, custom-designs learning experiences to fit the individualized needs of each student. That's like 25 people of different sizes and shapes wearing the exact same tuxedo, fitted perfectly to their own measurements. The goal is to make them all look as much like each other as possible. Personalized education is the quintessential 21st century nod to the industrial "Hierarchical Individual" education model and provides the rationale to keep it alive. It is saying that adults know exactly what all children need to know and when they need to know it but that we need a "delivery system" for the content and skills that takes individual differences into account. In the end, a personalized learning model may not be about the student at all but simply a way to sugar-coat a poison pill – an apt term to describe the obsolete, test-based, content-heavy education model that prevails across the globe.

> Personalized education assumes that an adult, like a tailor, custom-designs learning experiences to fit the individualized needs of each student.

Personal education, on the other hand, starts with the personal aptitude, skills, interests, and needs of individual students. Learning experiences are designed from the ground up to develop each individual student's potential to be the best at whatever that student wants to be best at. In a personal education model, the teacher and student are partners working together to first figure out and then implement a program where learning is a means to the larger goal of citizenship, human development, and self-actualization. Personal education has the added advantage in that students are able to connect emotionally with the subject at hand because of their personal interest in it. Not only does this make learning more meaningful but it is also a good way to ensure that students will be learning things they are more likely to use later on in their lives.

Not time-bound

The architecture of time may present an even greater challenge to real learning than the architecture of space. While space constraints are easier to find workarounds for, time constraints are like a straitjacket from which there is no escape. No matter how good a lesson may be, or how engaged students are in a lesson, the tyranny of the school bell instantly tears it all apart. Mihaly Csikszentmihalyi in his book, "Flow," talks about how we are our most creative selves only after we enter a state of "flow."[13] This requires a level of attention and commitment to a task that would be nearly impossible to achieve in the highly artificial and orchestrated environments of classrooms. As if this weren't enough of a barrier to creativity, we have the added assurance that even for those rare occasions in which students may be able to get into flow in a classroom, there is a certainty it will be broken by the school bell.

Schools have recognized that the 45-minute period is simply not enough time to do any work of a serious nature and many have gone to a block schedule model with 90-minute blocks of time dedicated to a particular class or lesson. This is a step in the right direction but has its own problems. The opposite of flow is disengagement and boredom. If the lesson being taught or learned is intrinsically uninteresting and boring, then extending it to 90 minutes does nothing to help students get into a state of flow.

> While space constraints are easier to find workarounds for, time constraints are like a straitjacket from which there is no escape.

What we are suggesting is a school day without periods.

---

[13] Flow: The Psychology of Optimal Experience by Mihaly Csikszentmihalyi. Harper & Row 1990

2 CHAPTER EIGHT PRINCIPLES THAT DEFINE THE NEW SCHOOL DESIGN PARADIGM

Figure 2-8: What most adults don't fully understand is that students, even at a very early age, are fully capable of directing their own learning. Another key learning fact is that the more "agency" a student has to make important decisions about what to learn and how to learn it, the more engaged he or she will be and the better the quality of the learning.
Shorecrest Early Childhood Center, St. Petersburg, Florida.

This will work only if it is combined with an individual learning plan for every student that provides every student with a clear roadmap of where he or she needs to be in any given area of expertise at the end of some defined period like a day, a week, a month, or a semester. The learning plan is co-created by the student and his or her teachers and is the only reference of progress. Think of an architectural office with 25 people in it. Everyone knows what they need to do and when they need to do it by. Everyone has some tasks that are more complicated than others, some that take longer and some that require partnering with others in the firm. Is there a bell that goes off at fixed intervals throughout the work day? Obviously, if it made sense to stop everyone cold in their tracks every 45 or 90 minutes so that they are forced to drop what they are doing and move onto another task, then this would be the way most businesses are run. Yes, we understand that schools aren't architectural offices but the work example illustrates the absurdity of making *any* group stop and start their work at fixed intervals regardless of what they are actually doing or how much time they actually need to properly execute the task at hand.

If the lesson being taught or learned is intrinsically uninteresting and boring, then extending it to 90 minutes does nothing to help students get into a state of flow.

Figure 2-9: Author Daniel Pink once asked, "When was the last time you spent any significant time with a group of individuals who were all the same age as you?" Age-based groupings don't make sense in the real world and make no sense in school either. It makes eminent sense to group students in ways that offer them the best opportunity to get a rich learning experience and not on the basis of their age. Spaces in school like this commons area provide opportunities for inter-age groupings in a way that grade-based classrooms don't. PK Yonge Developmental Research School at the University of Florida. Gainesville.

Self-Directed

The term "student-centered" is often used to imply self-direction. However, this term can lead to some confusion. To illustrate, let us look at a scenario where we observe a teacher sitting silently, passively observing or gently coaching as students are laboring hard on a multiplicity of assignments. On its face, this seems like a perfect description of what a student-centered learning activity looks like. Now let's assume that the work students are doing has been highly orchestrated by the teacher beforehand so that students are actually just carrying out the teacher's instructions even as they are hard at work.

Compare this to another scenario where the students are also engaged in work that, on its face, looks very similar to the above scenario. Except here, students worked together with the teacher and negotiated not only what they would work on but also how they would execute the assignment and for how long they would work on it. What we are saying is that student agency, the recognition by adults of their interests and preferences, is the secret to having them be truly engaged as learners.

> A personalized learning model may not be about the student at all but simply a way to sugar-coat a poison pill.

2 CHAPTER EIGHT PRINCIPLES THAT DEFINE THE NEW SCHOOL DESIGN PARADIGM

Figure 2-10: *Taking teachers out of classrooms they own and giving them, instead, an area where they can work and collaborate like professionals is probably one of the biggest game-changers when it comes to educational innovation. Collaboration that is continuous throughout the school day is far more effective than the isolated hour or two of group prep times that teachers normally have during any given week.*
PK Yonge Developmental Research School at the University of Florida. Gainesville.

Inter-Age

Strong as the structures around subject-based and classroom-based groupings are, they are easier to dismantle than age-based groupings in school. We have found no evidence that shows some intrinsic educational or human developmental value to organizing students by age and, yet, it is an age-old practice (no pun intended) that seems nearly impossible to break. Any parent with more than one child at home knows the benefits of having interaction between children of different ages. Such interactions benefit both the younger and older children in different ways. Yet, we see very little of this in schools. All this starts with the classroom. Once a decision is made to organize a fixed group of students within one small room with an adult, then it follows that we may as well group them by age for our own convenience as adults. It allows us to rationalize the uniform delivery of content and skills under the false premise that all students of a similar age need to and will progress at a similar pace developmentally

Student agency, the recognition by adults of their interests and preferences, is the secret to having them be truly engaged as learners.

if they are subjected to the same teaching practice. Even though we know this is patently wrong and that no two children are exactly alike, the fear is that the differences and learning difficulties will be even further exaggerated with a multi-age group. The fallacy to this argument is that we need not subject the multi-age group to the same teaching practice and, in fact, having a multi-age group of students only illustrates what we already know – that all children are different and they are different not only because they are not all the same age. With this realization, we can begin to

> Any parent with more than one child at home knows the benefits of having interaction between children of different ages.

rethink teaching itself and allow it to take a backseat as learning becomes front and center with students directing their own learning and also helping each other. This theory has been proven convincingly by Dr. Sugata Mitra with his hole in the wall experiments. These experiments show definitively that inter-age groups of students are perfectly capable of self-organizing even with the complete absence of adult supervision.[14]

Collaborative Teacher Teams

Why do we have an educational model in which one teacher is in charge of a fixed cohort of students organized by age? We have a one-word answer to that. The classroom. The moment you create a classroom and fill it with an age-based cohort of students, you also need them to have an adult supervisor – hence the teacher. That means, the rationale to have one teacher for 25 or 35 or even 15 students is really not one grounded in an education rationale, but one driven by the architecture of schools. Classroom = teacher + fixed number of same-age students.

We have compelling evidence that this system, which isolates teachers with students while preventing teachers from collaborating effectively with their peers, is actually a terrible one both from the teacher's and student's perspective.[15] Our idea is to move away from the classroom-based model to the learning community model in which teachers and students are not trapped in classrooms. Instead, multi-size and multi-age groupings of students can vary throughout the school day and the teacher-student ratio can also vary continuously to best accommodate the learning that is actually going on.[16]

Collaborative teacher teams have the advantage in that students have continuous access to a caring group of adults instead of having to primarily depend only on one classroom teacher. From the teachers' perspective, they will no longer be isolated from their peers but be able to collaborate with them to develop interesting and engaging multidisciplinary lessons. Socially also, teachers who can work in close collaboration with their peers are likely to be more professionally fulfilled and happy. All this translates into better student outcomes – not just with test scores but also in the areas that matter such as being more engaged and fulfilled, and happy.

> Collaborative teacher teams have the advantage in that students have continuous access to a caring group of adults instead of having to primarily depend only on one classroom teacher.

---

[14] Kids Can Teach Themselves. LIFT 2007. TED Talk. https://www.ted.com/talks/sugata_mitra_shows_how_kids_teach_themselves?language=en
[15] The Missing Link in School Reform, Carrie R. Leanna, Stanford Social Innovation Review 2011 https://www2.ed.gov/programs/slcp/2011progdirmtg/mislinkinrfm.pdf
[16] Blueprint for Tomorrow, Redesigning Schools for Student Centered Learning by Prakash Nair, Harvard Education Press, 2014

3 CHAPTER LIVE

"Live" covers all the aspects of the school experience that has to do with students in their individual and social milieu at school. It is also the realm that provides the greatest opportunities for emotional and spiritual growth and nourishment. Here are the areas we cover under the "live" category:

- Group collaboration
- Relaxing
- Meditating
- Physical fitness
- Socializing
- Eating
- Taking care of animals
- Gardening
- Community service

Group Collaboration

School provides the best milieu for students to learn about and practice teamwork. By and large, schools are institutions set up for individual achievement even when such achievement must be realized as part of a team. Students who work for the common good as a member of a team and benefit from the genius of the group will also hone the skills needed for success as adults. Consider again the top 10 skills for 2020

Figure 3-1: *Students who work for the common good as a member of a team and benefit from the genius of the group will also hone the skills needed for success as adults. Almost all the careers of the early and mid 21st century will require some level of team collaboration and so it is essential that these skills be acquired in school.*

discussed in Chapter Two. Notice how almost all of them will require teamwork. It is a safe bet that an integral part of the "life" that students will live outside school will require them to learn how to work as an integral member of a team toward some higher goal that would be beyond the reach of individuals and individual effort alone.

From the standpoint of designing spaces for group collaboration, we can think of a number of areas beyond the classroom where teams of students can work together. This could be small breakout areas for two students to work as a pair, a small group room for 5 to 8 students, a round cafe table, a comfortable couch seating arrangement, and even outdoor benches and tables for group work. Teachers do their best to encourage collaboration within their classrooms by grouping students around tables or combining desks but a small classroom is not an ideal environment for several groups of students to be simultaneously working together in teams.

3 CHAPTER LIVE

Figure 3-2: *It is never too early to teach students how to work in small groups. This shifts the focus of education from competition to collaboration, from obsessing about individual achievement according to some narrow measures of success such as test scores to a focus on team spirit, empathy and the appreciation of diversity.*
PK Yonge Developmental Research School at the University of Florida. Gainesville.

Relaxing

It is easy to dismiss the need to relax or "chill" as a luxury that schools cannot afford to give students. After all, students have enough time at home and on weekends and holidays to get in as much relaxation as they need so why should they also have such opportunities in schools? The answer lies in the way the human brain operates. Carl Zimmer wrote a provocative piece in Discover Magazine titled, *The Brain: Stop Paying Attention: Zoning Out Is a Crucial Mental State*. According to Zimmer, "Researchers say a wandering mind may be important to setting goals, making discoveries, and living a balanced life."[17] These are hardly the things that one must do exclusively at home and so it makes sense for schools to provide times and places for students to get a break and simply relax from what is usually a

> A small classroom is not an ideal environment for several groups of students to be simultaneously working together in teams.

---

[17] Carl Zimmer, "The Brain: Stop Paying Attention: Zoning Out is a Crucial Mental State", Discover Magazine, July-August 2009.

Figure 3-3: *Soft seats, beanbags, couches, armchairs, window seats and quiet areas away from active zones — preferably with connections to nature — are important ways in which schools can encourage and celebrate the notion of relaxation.*
Meadowlark School, Boulder Valley, Colorado.
Photo © Fred J. Fuhrmeister.

fully programmed school day.

Architecturally, soft seats, beanbags, couches, armchairs, window seats, and quiet areas away from active zones — preferably with connections to nature — are important ways in which schools can encourage and celebrate the notion of relaxation.

Meditating

Closely aligned with relaxing, meditating is also an activity that schools will do well to encourage in students. Once again, this may be something students can do just as well at home. However, given the increasingly complex and stressful world that our students will live in as adults, there is little question that the well-documented benefits of meditation will serve them well not only in school but throughout their lives.

The well-documented benefits of meditation will serve students well not only in school but throughout their lives.

Visitacion Valley Middle School first introduced Quiet Time (QT), a stress-reduction program as an optional activity, in the spring of 2007. Since starting the Quiet Time intervention, this school has achieved a 50% reduction in suspensions and 65% reduction in truancy.[18]

The good thing with meditation is that it can happen anywhere — yes, even in the classroom since it is a quiet "activity" that can benefit from being held in places which are acoustically separated from the adjoining areas.

Socializing

A teacher friend of ours tells the story of having an important group of foreign visitors to his class. The visitors observed several of his students engaged in an animated discussion and asked him what the students were so excited about — assuming, naturally, that he must have just concluded some provocative lecture or lesson. The teacher went up to the students, talked

Figures 3-4: *On good days, consider sending children to relax, work or socialize outside. The value of the outdoors as a place for relaxation is often overlooked by schools and school designers.*

Figure 3-5: *Given the increasingly complex and stressful world that our students will live in as adults, there is little question that the well-documented benefits of meditation will serve them well not only in school but throughout their lives. Meditation practice can work even when schools can't conjure up this kind of a magnificent setting, which is the top of a sandstone hill in Snow Canyon Utah! Photo © Aaron Hawkins.*

---

[18] Daily Meditation: A Bold Approach to Reducing Student Stress. Student behavior improved after implementing meditation techniques to relax students, promote a sense of well-being, and foster more-positive interactions. Edutopia. https://www.edutopia.org/stw-student-stress-meditation

3 CHAPTER LIVE

Figures 3-6: *As with most other elements of good design, variety is the key to creating schools in which students are able to socialize naturally and comfortably indoors and outdoors.*
PK Yonge Developmental Research School at the University of Florida. Gainesville.

briefly with them and came back to announce, "No, they are not discussing school work. They are just excited about the narrow win of our local baseball team in the playoffs last night." To our teacher friend, this was a completely natural thing for his students to do. He did not start with the assumption that the sanctity of the classroom would be destroyed if "real" learning were not happening all the time. He realized that being social is, in fact, an essential element of real learning. Indeed, social skills have often been cited as a leading determinant of career and life success. It is, therefore, incumbent on us to ensure that students are given sufficient opportunities to be social while in school.

Almost every place in school should be designed from the perspective of its viability as a good place to be social. There is great variability in the need for social spaces, and students will naturally gravitate to areas for socializing that best meet not only their personality but also who they are with and the nature of the social activity. Social areas can vary from high-energy cafes to quiet study areas, from amphitheater-style seating indoors and outdoors to breakout areas adjacent to learning studios. As with most other elements of good design, variety is the key to creating schools in which students are able to socialize naturally and comfortably.

> Social skills have often been cited as a leading determinant of career and life success.

Figure 3-7: *Places to eat in school no longer have to be purely utilitarian and institutional in the way that school cafeterias have traditionally been. Eating places can be used beyond lunch periods and throughout the school day and for after school activities if they are set up to resemble cafes. Suitable, mobile furniture, easy to clean surfaces, good acoustic treatment, views to nature and outdoor connections are qualities to look for in student cafes.*
Summit Middle School, Boulder Valley, Colorado.

Eating

Eating is, of course, very important, especially for children who need to consume food more often than adults. Thus, school cafeterias are designed to deal exclusively with their charge of feeding students as a way to sustain them physically. This narrow and limited view of eating that most schools adopt ignores the reality that, throughout human history, eating has been as much a social activity as it it has been about physical sustenance. Beyond the general socializing that happens throughout the school day, we subscribe to the notion of creating cafes in schools where such socializing can happen over a beverage, snack or meal. This approach will also break down the idea of setting strict times for meals as if students will all be hungry on demand and only when the school determines it. It is our contention that students should have access to food and beverages throughout the school day and that they should be able to use eating time to socialize with their peers and also seamlessly continue whatever schoolwork they are interested in continuing either alone or with friends.

>
> Students should have access to food and beverages throughout the school day.

Figure 3-8: *Gardening with children has many benefits. It connects them with nature and helps them breathe fresh air, gets them interested in fruits and vegetables making them more likely to eat them, gets them away from the computer screen, involves physical activity and makes them more environmentally conscious. This picture shows children participating in a tree-planting event sponsored by Growing Together in California. Photo © Jason Clary. Growing Together: Mallika Nair, Founder.*

From a design standpoint, we recommend that schools decentralize the eating function even when they are operating out of one central cooking kitchen. There are a number of ways to do this including the location of satellite cafes instead of (or in addition to) one large central cafe and also allowing students the option of eating in outdoor eating areas either adjacent to the cafe or in other shaded areas — preferably in natural settings. We have discussed this subject in greater detail in our book, "The Language of School Design."[19]

Gardening

Adults lament the fact that so much of our childrens' time is spent in front of a screen — these include phones, tablets, computers, and TV. This has come at the price of them spending more and more time indoors. By and large, schooling is also an indoor activity, but we recommend that every

Integrate the garden into your cafeteria, into your biology class, or gym class, make healthy living and eating a visible priority at your school.

---

[19] The Language of School Design by Prakash Nair, Randall Fielding and Jeffrey Lackney. Third Edition. 2013. Designshare

effort be made to move learning activities outdoors. One natural fit for an outdoor activity is gardening. All schools should make an attempt to have a kitchen garden. Where land and weather permit, schools can also lead efforts to build and maintain community gardens.

This is an activity that students tend to enjoy. It also comes with numerous ancillary benefits such as breathing fresh air, becoming more environmentally conscious, becoming more likely to eat healthy, organic fruits and vegetables, becoming more aware of good health and nutrition, being more physically active and learning about the benefits of teamwork and community building.

> There are various ways in which taking care of animals in school can be a good thing for students.

Look for partnerships with local organizations to help your school start a vegetable garden. In the words of a Montreal-based organic gardening group, "Imagine your schoolyard transformed, filled with fruit trees, berries and perennial vegetables. Transform your underused space into a positive space to connect and learn about plants and nature.

Children get to learn about nature, all while learning to care for the plants and each other. They discover where food comes from, how it grows and taste the fruit of their labors. Treat their sweet tooth to the real sweets of nature, strawberries, raspberries, and blueberries. Plant a fruit tree in your school yard. Integrate the garden into your cafeteria, into your biology class, or gym class, make healthy living and eating a visible priority at your school."[20]

In a similar vein, Growing Together, an Oakland, CA-based nonprofit organization, provides support for underserved communities and schools using organic gardening as a tool for education, healthy living, and community building.[21]

Taking Care of Animals

Figure 3-9: *Taking care of animals in school can be a good thing for students. It teaches them empathy, responsibility and discipline, and the bonding with animals that children naturally enjoy.*
Photo © Joni Mulvaney.

---

[20] Urban Seedling, Montreal, CA. https://www.urbanseedling.com/about/
[21] http://www.growingtogetherproject.org/

Figure 3-10: *Physical fitness goes beyond formal sports and is really a lifestyle in which people live active as opposed to sedentary lives. A commitment to the physical health of students will require schools to provide the proper indoor and outdoor facilities for formal and informal physical activities. Of course this needs to be supported by a schedule that provides adequate times during each school day when students can get up and move as opposed to spending excessive amounts of time sitting in classrooms.*

From having goldfish, hamsters, and bunnies in class to maintaining a chicken coop or even managing a small petting zoo, there are various ways in which taking care of animals in school can be a good thing for students. It teaches them empathy, responsibility, and discipline, and the bonding with animals that children naturally enjoy.

Despite their obvious benefits and the great affinity that children tend to have with animals, programs where children get to work with or take care of animals is the exception rather than the rule. The Ballarat Grammar School Farm Program is one worthy of emulating. Here, students spend most of their 4th grade year working on an active farm. This program shows how much of the learning that we believe can only happen in a classroom is actually better delivered in nature where students are breathing fresh air, learning valuable life skills, being more active physically and taking care of animals.

Physical Fitness

"Physical inactivity is a leading cause of disease and disability, warns WHO. … Sedentary lifestyles increase all causes of mortality, double the risk of cardiovascular diseases, diabetes, and obesity, and increase the risks of colon cancer, high blood pressure, osteoporosis, lipid disorders, depression and anxiety."[22]

Being physically fit represents a lifestyle more than just doing exercise. Schools need to emphasize the value of physical fitness from a very early age. We are fully in favor of the physical fitness programs at most schools — much of it delivered within indoor gymnasiums,

> **Being physically fit represents a lifestyle more than just doing exercise. Schools need to emphasize the value of physical fitness from a very early age.**

---

[22] Physical inactivity a leading cause of disease and disability, warns WHO. http://www.who.int/mediacentre/news/releases/release23/en/

Figure 3-11:
*Community service provides students with the opportunity to become active members of their community and has a lasting, positive impact on society at large. Community service or volunteerism enables students to acquire life skills and knowledge, as well as provide a service to those who need it most.
Photo © Eric Parthum .
Growing Together.*

some in playgrounds and some on athletic tracks, sports fields, and swimming pools. That means a commitment to the physical health of students will require schools to provide the proper indoor and outdoor facilities for formal and informal physical activities.

We subscribe to all manner of activities that keep students active and healthy. However, we would also like to point to some other ways in which to view physical fitness. This includes limiting the time that students spend sitting on chairs by having them stand and move around often during the school day — not in a forced manner but as a natural part of the activities they are engaged in. Learning Community-based models of school design will naturally involve more movement and physical activity in students than classroom-based models.

Community Service

We believe that it is essential for students to be given opportunities to serve their communities. Such opportunities can be designed in an age-appropriate manner. Done correctly, community service will not seem coercive but feel natural and become an important part of each student's education. For students to fully benefit from this experience, they need to be given a say in what they do, who they help, and how much time they will spend doing community service.

"Engaging in community service provides students with the opportunity to become active members of their community and has a lasting, positive impact on society at large. Community

> Done correctly, community service will not seem coercive but feel natural and become an important part of each student's education.

> Subjects, an artificial way to segment learning, allows the school day to be broken up into bite-sized chunks of time.

service or volunteerism enables students to acquire life skills and knowledge, as well as provide a service to those who need it most."[23]

All the activities listed in this chapter are probably offered by most schools around the world. However, we would argue that schools see these activities at best as peripheral and, at worst, as a distraction to "real" learning. Of course, the thesis of this book is that there can be no richer learning than that provided by life. We maintain that schools should be, first and foremost, about letting children live a good life and, from that experience, extract all the important lessons they will use throughout their own lives as they transition from being children and adolescents to young people and adults. In John Dewey's words, "Education is not preparation for life; education is life itself."

---

[23] Why is Community Service Important? Florida National University, April 8, 2013. https://www.fnu.edu/community-service-important/

CHAPTER 4
PLAY

By some measures, play is quickly becoming the dominant form of learning in this century. From a very early age, children use play as a simulation of life itself. Think about these characteristics of spontaneous play – this list applies as much to a game of chess as it does to soccer. 1) It is natural; 2) it is dynamic; 3) it is creative; 4) it requires strategy; 5) it helps you learn from mistakes; and 6) it is engaging and exciting. From a learning perspective, play represents the very essence of what we would want the whole school experience to be. Here are the areas that we cover in the "play" category:

> From a learning perspective, play represents the very essence of what we would want the whole school experience to be.

- Social games
- Games with manipulatives
- Physical activity play/sports
- Creative play with different materials
- Computer games
- Playing in nature

Figure 4-1: *In some cases, such social games can even have a physical component of movement and exercise such as when children play on a giant outdoor chess board.*

4 CHAPTER PLAY

Figure 4-2: *Role playing could be an extremely effective way to teach many humanities subjects but also in the sciences where students could play-act the roles of their favorite heroes.*

Social Games

Social games fall into a few categories such as[24]:

1. **Card games, board games, and games of mental agility like chess.** While these games are usually associated with the indoors, efforts should be made to use as many outdoor areas as possible for these kinds of social games. In some cases, such social games can even have a physical component of movement and exercise such as when children play on a giant outdoor chess board.

2. **Role-Playing.** "Players assume the roles of characters in a fictional setting. Players take responsibility for acting out these roles within a narrative, either through literal acting or through a process of structured decision-making of character development."[25] Clearly, such role-playing could be an extremely effective way to teach many humanities subjects but also in the sciences where students could play-act the roles of their favorite heroes. From a school design standpoint, such play-acting opportunities should be available not only in the more formal setting of a school's auditorium, but also in other less formal settings like the common areas adjacent to learning studios within a learning community.

Games with manipulatives

"Manipulative play refers to activities where children move, order, turn or screw items to make them fit. It allows children to take control of their world by mastering the objects they use. It is often solitary, but when sufficient resources are provided it can also be a cooperative activity. Manipulative equipment can help children to:

   a. Practice making decisions
   b. Learn about size, shape, weight, length, height
   c. Learn about sequence, comparison, order, patterns, colors, textures
   d. Learn to analyse and solve problems
   e. Develop concentration and perseverance
   f. Learn about cause and effect.[26]

> Manipulative play allows children to take control of their world by mastering the objects they use.

---

[24] Social Gaming. Wikipedia. https://en.wikipedia.org/wiki/Social_gaming
[25] Ibid
[26] Education.Govt.NZ. Play idea: Manipulative play - Mahi ā-ringa. https://education.govt.nz/early-childhood/teaching-and-learning/learning-tools-and-resources/play-ideas/manipulative-play/

4 CHAPTER PLAY

Figure 4-3: *Manipulative play allows children to take control of their world by mastering the objects they use. It is often solitary, but when sufficient resources are provided it can also be a cooperative activity. Schools need to provide sufficient space for free movement for children engaged in manipulative play. Elementary School at American School of Bombay, Mumbai.*

Play with manipulatives requires areas in the school to be set up properly with adequate storage to put things away when they are not in use. Some manipulatives work best when used on tables, so some of these would be handy and others work well on the floor.

Figure 4-6: *Some kinds of fitness need special equipment like this equipment and weight room that is, logically, placed adjacent to the gym. Some sporting activities while they happen outside the school building such as football and rowing, will also require an indoor physical fitness component which makes facilities like this important. In cases where schools cannot afford professional facilities like this, it is valuable to create user-agreements with community fitness centers that tend to be used sparingly during the school day. This will help level the playing field for students who may be attending schools with fewer resources.*

4 CHAPTER PLAY

Figure 4-4, 4-5: *Indoor gymnasiums are versatile places where, in addition to formal sports like basketball, volleyball and badminton, a variety of physical activities can take place, including cheerleading practice, gymnastics, jogging, dancing, dodge ball, etc. Gyms can also have a section with a climbing wall. Schools that recognize the value of physical activity will ensure that their indoor gymnasiums are used to the greatest extent possible. We subscribe to the idea that it is OK to use gymnasiums as multipurpose spaces for performances and other large gatherings but only if it doesn't negatively impact the school's athletic program.*

Physical Activity Play/Sports

This represents the kind of activities that can happen indoors in gymnasiums or outdoors on playfields. It covers the whole range of physical activities that exercise the large muscle groups from drills and games to participation in organized individual and team sports. Swimming (both recreational and competitive) would fall under this category. It provides key health benefits while developing an important life skill. While not every school can afford the full range of physical activities that students can benefit from, they should make every effort to connect with local partners to work out shared arrangements for the use of community facilities like gymnasiums and swimming pools.

Creative Play with Different Materials

While manipulatives refer to components that are specifically designed to enhance particular learning skills, children should also have times when they are encouraged to find creative applications indoors and outdoors for everyday materials like paper, wood, metal, cloth, rocks, sand, and so on. Building a

sand castle or a paper plane are examples of creative play with different materials. Here are some examples of natural materials that can be used for creative play: "Pine cones of different sizes, big feathers, loofahs, pumice (boil to keep clean), dried gourds, lemons or oranges, sheepskins, balls of wool, large leaves, large shells, coconut shells, rose petals, bark, lei, sticks, stones, driftwood, small cloth bags containing lavender, rosemary or thyme."[27]

Computer Games

There is no question that games like Minecraft have children all over the world playing on the computer obsessively and compulsively to the exclusion of almost anything else. It is up to parents to find ways to moderate such obsessions or even addictions by limiting the amount of time children can spend online while, at the same time, introducing them to other, preferably outdoor, activities. Keeping aside the addictive potential of video games which is, obviously, unhealthy, there is evidence that game-playing, when done in moderation, has many benefits. Here are six benefits identified by the TeachThought Staff who claim that, "playing online games may be something which can enhance a child's learning and development."[28]

Figure 4-9: *There is evidence that computer game-playing, when done in moderation, has many benefits. In fact, playing online games may be something that can enhance a child's learning and development. Rather than fight the urge that students have to play computer games, schools can create comfortable zones with ergonomic furniture (preferably with access to daylight and outside views) to make learning via games creative, immersive and engaging.*

1. Increases A Child's Memory Capacity
2. Computer & Simulation Fluency
3. Helps With Fast Strategic Thinking & Problem-Solving
4. Develops Hand-Eye Coordination
5. Beneficial Specifically For Children With Attention Disorders
6. Skill-Building (e.g., map reading)

But gaming isn't the lonely or nerdy activity that many adults assume it is. In fact, there is a major social dimension to computer games that schools can embrace by sensibly integrating it into the curriculum itself. For example, Minecraft is now being used in

Keeping aside the addictive potential of video games which is, obviously, unhealthy, there is evidence that game-playing, when done in moderation, has many benefits.

---

[27] Education.Govt.NZ. Play idea: Manipulative play - Mahi ā-ringa. https://education.govt.nz/early-childhood/teaching-and-learning/learning-tools-and-resources/play-ideas/manipulative-play/
[28] Six basic benefits of game-based learning. https://teachthought.com/technology/6-basic-benefits-of-game-based-learning/

Figure 4-7: *Children should have times when they are encouraged to find creative applications indoors and outdoors for everyday materials. In fact, the less "designed" the materials are, the more imagination children will use to make them usable and incorporate them into creative activities.*

schools around the world. "Minecraft is all about building—crafting and sharing, sharing and crafting."[29] Talking about Minecraft Edu, here is what Fast Company says, "The 'mod' lets teachers adapt Minecraft for the classroom, enabling them to write assignments, create boundaries, and guide their students to create together. As game-based learning expert Alan Gershenfeld says in a recent issue of Scientific American, 'not only is Minecraft immersive and creative, but it is an excellent platform for making almost any subject area more engaging.'"[30]

Playing in Nature

At the other end of the spectrum, far from the virtual worlds our children inhabit on the computer, there is the learning bounty of nature that remains sadly underutilized by most schools. This is a real problem because, "More and more children today have less and less contact with the natural world. And this is having a huge impact on their health and development."[31] In his book, "Last Child in the Woods", author Richard Louv gives this deprivation a name. He calls it, "Nature Deficit Disorder."

A Guardian article titled, "Why our Children Need to Get Outside and Engage with Nature" notes that "Obesity is perhaps the most visible symptom of the lack of such play, but literally dozens of studies from around the world show regular time outdoors produces significant improvements in attention deficit hyperactivity disorder, learning ability, creativity and mental, psychological and emotional wellbeing.

Just five minutes of "green exercise" can produce rapid improvements in mental well-being and self-esteem, with the greatest benefits experienced by the young, according to a study this year at the University of Essex.

Free and unstructured play in the outdoors boosts problem-solving skills, focus, and self-discipline. Socially, it improves

---

[29] Is Minecraft the Future of Social Networking? Fast Company. https://www.fastcompany.com/3026146/is-minecraft-the-future-of-social-networking
[30] Ibid
[31] Why Our Children Need to Get Outside and Engage with Nature. The Guardian. https://www.theguardian.com/lifeandstyle/2010/aug/16/childre-nature-outside-play-health

cooperation, flexibility, and self-awareness. Emotional benefits include reduced aggression and increased happiness. "Children will be smarter, better able to get along with others, healthier and happier when they have regular opportunities for free and unstructured play in the out-of-doors," concluded one authoritative study published by the American Medical Association in 2005."

> More and more children today have less and less contact with the natural world. And this is having a huge impact on their health and development.

The Guardian article goes on to quote Stephen Moss, naturalist, broadcaster and author, who says, "Nature is a tool to get children to experience not just the wider world, but themselves. So climbing a tree is about learning how to take responsibility for yourself, and how – crucially – to measure risk for yourself. Falling out of a tree is a very good lesson in risk and reward.'"[32]

We recommend that schools consciously set aside at least two hours each day for children to engage in nature-based outdoor activities — preferably unstructured play. Weather should not be a detriment to going outside. There is a saying that all schools should adopt, "There is no such thing as bad weather, only inappropriate clothing."

Figure 4-8: *Free and unstructured play in the outdoors boosts problem-solving skills, focus and self-discipline. Socially, it improves cooperation, flexibility, and self-awareness. Emotional benefits include reduced aggression and increased happiness. Children will be smarter, better able to get along with others, healthier and happier when they have regular opportunities for free and unstructured play in the outdoors.*

The best way for children to experience the outdoors is to be doing things that people naturally do outdoors like farming, taking care of animals and so on but even on more formal playgrounds, we would suggest replacing the predictable plastic slides, swings and jungle-gyms with natural landscape elements that allow for more spontaneous, social and creative play.

> Just five minutes of "green exercise" can produce rapid improvements in mental well-being and self-esteem, with the greatest benefits experienced by the young.

---

[32] Ibid

CHAPTER 5
ENGAGE

"Engage" is about the more familiar things we normally associate with school, primarily academic growth and achievement. Ironically, by focusing so heavily on academics, schools often lose the opportunity to showcase learning not as an end unto itself, but in service of some higher purpose. The hard and, sometimes, uninspiring, work students need to do in this realm can only be fully rationalized for its long-term value when students can see direct connections between theory and practice and understand why the academic aspects of school will benefit them at a very personal level. For real learning to occur, benefits to students need to extend far beyond the desire to please a teacher or do well on an exam. Let us keep referring back to Prof. Elmore's definition of learning, which requires students to "consciously" engage with an activity as a prelude to "modifying" their worldview and "learning" something. Here are the areas covered in this book under the "Engage" category:

- Direct Instruction
- Reading
- Research
- Experimentation
- Cooperative Learning
- Entrepreneurship

Figure 5-1: *Direct instruction can take the form of brief lectures. Done well, it is an effective way to communicate essential information that students can then use to continue their learning. This picture shows how a good teacher in a good environment can hold children's attention and keep them engaged.*

Figure 5-2: *In this example, direct instruction is delivered to a small group in a setting that is clearly designed for student work. The teacher uses a rolling whiteboard to give some basic information along with short instructions in order to give students the direction they need to develop their own ideas and work in small teams or independently.*
Academy of the Holy Names, Tampa, Florida Middle School iLab.

- Presentations
- Internships
- Projects

Direct Instruction

There will always be room for formal instruction, although the value of such instruction will depend on whether or not students are there by choice or because they are forced to attend. There is a myth that "direct instruction" is about a teacher lecturing to a classroom full of students. This method of direct instruction is dictated by the design of the school where groups of students are isolated in classrooms with one adult. Once this model is broken and the learning environment no longer dictates that a teacher must always be present with a fixed cohort of students, the word "direct instruction" can take on a whole new meaning. A teacher could be helping a smaller group of students — perhaps as small as three or four students or even working one-on-one with an individual student doing what he or she may have done in front of a classroom with 25 or 35 students. The form of instruction remains the same but the results are likely to be far better. Under the model of direct instruction where only those students who need the extra help and guidance from a teacher get it, there is a greater engagement on the part of students,

> The teacher should be able to tailor his or her lesson in a manner that will best benefit the individual students who are participating in that "class."

5 CHAPTER ENGAGE

Figure 5-3, 5-4: *There are few learning activities that are more beneficial to students than reading. However, children rarely get to read for pleasure in schools and there aren't too many comfortable places where they could get lost in a book. Reading used to be the domain of libraries but, with comfortable furnishings and sufficient down time from other subjects, students should be able to read anywhere in school – and especially in their primary academic areas like classrooms and learning communities.*
Anne Frank Inspire Academy, San Antonio, Texas.

Figure 5-5: *The importance of research as an essential life skill has increased greatly with the glut of information flooding all manner of media. Now, more than ever before, students need to be able to distinguish between fact and propaganda and learn how to look for multiple sources of data to back up information that they find online. Research using wireless laptops can now happen anytime, anywhere and be a part of any subject or curriculum. iLab at Horace Greeley High School, Chappaqua, NY.*

and the lesson no longer feels mass produced. That is because the teacher is able to tailor his or her lesson in a manner that will best benefit the individual students who are participating in that "class." Another important change of a direct instruction model that doesn't depend on being delivered in a classroom to a captive audience is that it is also free from the schedule constraints that traditional school "periods" impose. Under the model that we are describing, a direct instruction "lesson" may be as short as a couple of minutes or an hour or more, depending on what is being taught and what the learners' needs are.

Reading

There are few activities in school that are more beneficial to students than reading. Writer Lana Winter-Hébert talks about 10 benefits that justify reading as an important daily activity for everyone.[33] Here is her list:

1. Mental Stimulation
2. Stress Reduction
3. Knowledge
4. Vocabulary Expansion
5. Memory Improvement
6. Stronger Analytical Thinking Skills
7. Improved Focus and Concentration
8. Better Writing Skills
9. Tranquility
10. Free Entertainment

---

[33] 10 Benefits of Reading: Why You Should Read Every Day by Lana Winter-Hébert. Lifehack
https://www.lifehack.org/articles/lifestyle/10-benefits-reading-why-you-should-read-everyday.html

5 CHAPTER ENGAGE

Figure 5-6, 5-7: Experimentation can and should, of course, happen with the hard sciences that students are engaged in but also in areas such as art, language, theater, music, math, gardening, food preparation, and sport.

For all its benefits, there are few places in most schools where the environments are made conducive to this important activity. Of course, school libraries are an exception, but how much time do students actually get to curl up comfortably with a good book in their school libraries? We believe that schools should offer a variety of reading-friendly places both indoors and outdoors that students can access throughout the school day. Similarly, students should have free and ready access to a variety of reading materials and not be limited to so-called "assigned" books that take away the joy of reading and make it a chore rather than the pleasurable activity it should be.

Research

The importance of research as an essential life skill has increased greatly with the glut of information flooding all manner of media. Now, more than ever before, students need to be able to distinguish between fact and propaganda and learn how to look for multiple sources of data to back up information that they find online. Here are seven reasons why it is important for students to have time in school to not just learn how to do research, but to actually become researchers.[34] Research is:

1. A tool for building knowledge and efficient learning
2. A means to understand various issues

---
[34] 7 Reasons Why Research Is Important by Leann Zarah. Owlcation -- . https://owlcation.com/academia/Why-Research-is-Important-Within-a

3. An aid to business success
4. A way to disprove lies and support truths
5. A means to find, gauge, and seize opportunities
6. A Seed to Love Reading, Writing, Analyzing, and Sharing Valuable Information
7. Nourishment and Exercise for the Mind

> What DaVinci showed is that experimentation is at the heart of real creativity and that new ideas only emerge when one can push past the comfortable boundaries of what we know and are brave enough to look for what lies beyond.

This raises important questions for schools and the way in which they are designed. Where, when, and how can research be made an essential and integral part of every school day?

Experimentation

An experiment refers to a series of steps one might take to prove or disprove a hypothesis. In schools, the term and the work associated with the word "experiment" has been co-opted by the science lab. However, experimentation is something we do all the time. It reflects any effort we put in to try something different where the outcome is uncertain. Experimentation is about disturbing the status quo to observe the results. It is this broader view of experimentation that we believe schools need to take. Students need to be encouraged to try new things, make mistakes, learn from those mistakes and try again. Experimentation can and should, of course, happen with the hard sciences that students are engaged in but also in areas such as art, language, theater, music, math, gardening, food preparation, and sport.

We often like to point to Leonardo DaVinci as the ultimate experimenter. What DaVinci showed is that experimentation is at the heart of real creativity and that new ideas only emerge when one can push past the comfortable boundaries of what we know and become brave enough to look for what lies beyond. In the design of schools, we need to instill a culture of risk-taking and experimentation that extends beyond science and "infects" all subject areas.

Cooperative Learning

Cooperative learning is now a well regarded and accepted form of learning — meaning that educators and educational researchers have endorsed it as a method of learning that is preferable to the alternative, which is individualistic and competitive learning. "Unlike individual learning, which can be competitive in nature, students learning cooperatively can capitalize on one another's resources and skills (asking one another for information, evaluating one another's ideas, monitoring one another's work, etc)."[35]

Cooperative learning requires two or more students to work together toward some common goal. The nature of the work will vary depending on the problem that the group has been engaged in solving and the ancillary tasks needed to be accomplished. While cooperative learning can happen in classrooms, they are not ideal for team and group work for the following reasons.

> Unlike individual learning, which can be competitive in nature, students learning cooperatively can capitalize on one another's resources and skills.

---

[35] Cooperative Learning. Wikipedia. https://en.wikipedia.org/wiki/Cooperative_learning

Figure 5-8: *Cooperative learning is now a well regarded and accepted form of learning — meaning that educators and educational researchers have endorsed it as a method of learning that is preferable to the alternative, which is individualistic and competitive learning. Unlike individual learning, which can be competitive in nature, students learning cooperatively can capitalize on one another's resources and skills (asking one another for information, evaluating one another's ideas, monitoring one another's work, etc).*

Classrooms, generally, are not big enough to accommodate all the students in a cooperative learning mode because of the way in which furniture will need to be rearranged with sufficient space between the various groups.

Cooperative learning activities tend to involve more interaction between team members than might be the case under the individualistic learning model. This will increase noise levels in the classroom, which will militate against the quality of the learning.

When students are working in a team towards the solution of some larger problem, different members of the team may be assigned different tasks to complete. That will necessitate students having access to many more modes of learning than may be possible to introduce into the limited confines of a classroom environment.

For the above reasons, cooperative learning activities that require group collaboration are best accomplished in learning communities as opposed to classrooms. Learning communities offer multiple modes of learning and more space to move

Figure 5-9: *Student entrepreneurs have a wide range of opportunities to express themselves. For example, they can start small incubator businesses on the school grounds that serve the local community, they can promote high quality student art projects by organizing exhibitions and sale of student work, they can create "branded" school products and market them to the larger community. Graphic adapted from REAL Entrepreneur.*

around in, thereby serving as a more effective environment for cooperative learning.

Entrepreneurship

"Most institutions do not teach what should be the centerpiece of a contemporary education: entrepreneurship, the capacity to not only start companies but also to think creatively and ambitiously."[36] Stuck doing boring, repetitive tasks and regurgitating information that they are forced to memorize, it's no wonder that many otherwise brilliant minds are put in a straitjacket in school.

Student entrepreneurs have a wide range of opportunities to express themselves. For example, they can start small incubator businesses on the school grounds that serve the local community, they can promote high quality student art projects by

---

[36] Why Schools Should Teach Entrepreneurship by Florina Rodov and Sabrina Truong. Entrepreneur
https://www.entrepreneur.com/article/245038

Figure 5-10: *In order for students to get a head start on becoming effective communicators, they need to hone their presentation skills as early in their lives as possible. Spaces need to be set up throughout the school building for formal and impromptu presentations with and without the benefit of technology to be conducted effortlessly by students of all ages.*

organizing exhibitions and sale of student work, they can create "branded" school products and market them to the larger community. In Chapter 10, we have shown a proposed design for a "Young Entrepreneurs' Studio," a physical space in which student entrepreneurs can learn to plan, start and operate a real business.

"Maya Penn, a 13-year-old TED talker, sells her own knit scarves and hats online and donates a percentage of her proceeds to nonprofits. Sixteen-year-old prodigy Erik Finman, who recalls a teacher telling him to drop out and work at McDonald's, founded the video-chat tutoring program Botangle and the startup Intern for a Day, which connects companies with potential interns who work for a day on a project that constitutes a vocational audition."[37]

> Stuck doing boring, repetitive tasks and regurgitating information that they are forced to memorize, it's no wonder that many otherwise brilliant minds are put in a straitjacket in school.

Compare these kinds of activities and achievements to what tends to happen during a typical school day. Isn't it time to rethink how we organize time, space, and curriculum so that young talent that might otherwise be squandered or crushed can thrive and flourish in school?

---

[37] Ibid

Presentations

At VEGA school in New Delhi, students as young as 9 and 10 lead visitors on a comprehensive tour of the school. After the tour, they sit visitors down to a full blown presentation of their goals, accomplishments, and challenges. VEGA students are no different than young children their age at any other school, except that, here, they are given an opportunity to be their own spokespersons. The confidence that comes from this kind of early exposure to public presentations will allow VEGA students to graduate with an essential life skill that will serve them well not only in professional settings but in personal and social situations as well.

> In order for students to get a head start on becoming effective communicators, they need to hone their presentation skills as early in their lives as possible.

George Torok provides six specific reasons why strong presentation skills are important as follows:[38]

1. They contribute to individual success
2. They are an important determinant in business success
3. They reduce the stress that most people suffer when having to publicly present their ideas
4. They help hone the message when under severe time constraints
5. They are an important trait for good leadership
6. They can positively shape both public image and opinion

In order for students to get a headstart on becoming effective communicators, they need to hone their presentation skills as early in their lives as possible, as VEGA students are doing.[39] From a design standpoint, spaces need to be set up throughout the school building so that both formal and impromptu presentations with and without the benefit of technology can be conducted effortlessly by students of all ages and by teachers as well.

Internships

Internships provide the best opportunity for students to get exposed to the real world of work and to see how well the skills they developed in school will hold up in that setting. Students who come from schools that practice John Dewey's dictum that schools are not preparation for life but are life itself, will adapt more easily to the world of internships — but they, too, will benefit in many ways from their learning to the world outside.

Here is CNN's take on why Internships are important.[40]

"Besides getting a foot in the door with a potential

> Internships provide the best opportunity for students to get exposed to the real world of work and to see how well the skills they developed in school will hold up in that setting.

---

[38] Why Are Presentation Skills Important by George Torok
http://www.torok.com/articles/presentation/WhyArePresentationSkillsImportant.html
[39] See Chapter 10 for a more detailed write up about Vega Schools
[40] Why are internships so important? By Beth Braccio Hering, CareerBuilder.com. April 14, 2010 11:09 a.m. EDT CNN.
http://www.cnn.com/2010/LIVING/worklife/04/14/cb.why.internships.important/index.html

employer and looking good on a résumé, internships have other advantages:

1. The opportunity to "test drive" a career (Would I be happier in marketing or advertising? Am I more comfortable working with patients or in a lab?)
2. Chances to network
3. Establishing relationships with mentors
4. Possible college credit or certification
5. An introduction to the field's culture and etiquette (Are clients addressed by their first name? Are jeans appropriate for Casual Friday?)
6. Accumulating new skills
7. Gaining a "real world" perspective on an occupation (How much overtime do employees really work? How much time is spent behind a desk versus in the field?)

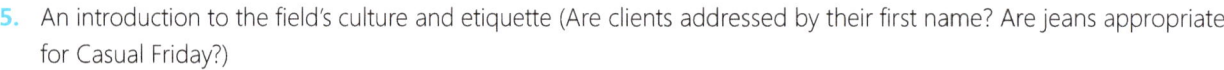

> The fact that students who go away on internships need to come back to more comfortable, student-centered learning environments simply adds more weight to our argument that we need to design schools differently than we have been doing for more than a hundred years.

From a design standpoint, one might imagine that having students go away on internships outside school has no impact on the design of spaces within the school itself. We don't agree. Students who experience the modern workplace will feel even more disconnected with schools that look and feel like the cells and bells model that they may otherwise be able to tolerate. We have provided numerous reasons throughout this book why schools for today and tomorrow need to look and feel different. The fact that students who go away on internships need to come back to more comfortable, student-centered learning environments simply adds more weight to our argument that we need to design schools differently than we have been doing for more than a hundred years.

Projects

It is not a hard case to make that *all* learning in school should be "project" based. After all, what is the real, sustained value of simply "learning" disconnected facts and figures with no real context or an opportunity to apply that learning? Brain research tells us that while we may be able to recollect information for the period of time it takes to regurgitate it on an exam, the brain does not retain information that ceases to have direct use or value. This makes the vast majority of the "stuff" learned in school useless and unnecessary, since most of it will be forgotten in due course.

Projects, on the other hand, can provide an immediate, relevant, and engaging vehicle to apply learning and thereby test its value and also ensure its longevity. "Project based learning helps students develop skills for living in a knowledge-based, highly technological society. The old-school model of passively learning

> It is not a hard case to make that all learning in school should be "project" based. After all, what is the real, sustained value of simply "learning" disconnected facts and figures with no real context or an opportunity to apply that learning?

Figure 5-11: *From a space design perspective, the primary driver for a school that will be able to successfully deliver a project based curriculum is that it will contain more areas for hands-on learning. In other words, less theory and more practice will require more places for that practice. Hands-on learning does not mean only science labs and makerspaces but also spaces like this where research, collaboration and hands-on, multi-disciplinary project work is possible.*
Mid Pacific Institute, Hawaii.

facts and reciting them out of context is no longer sufficient to prepare students to survive in today's world."[41]

From a space design perspective, the primary driver for a school that will be able to successfully deliver a project-based curriculum is that it will contain more areas for hands-on learning. In other words, less theory and more practice will require more places for that practice. Hands-on learning does not mean only science labs and "makerspaces." We believe that most places in the school building, including outdoor learning areas, should lend themselves to active learning, meaning there should be large work surfaces, wet areas, durable floors, high ceilings where needed, access to relevant equipment, storage and exhibit spaces with proper daylighting, acoustic separation, and technology.

---

[41] Why Is Project-Based Learning Important? The many merits of using project-based learning in the classroom. EDUTOPIA OCTOBER 19, 2007
https://www.edutopia.org/project-based-learning-guide-importance

CHAPTER 6
CREATE

Create is what schools for today and tomorrow are about. Just pause for a moment and contemplate the billions of pages of information, games, music, services, courses, and specific tools for skill building that are available online. Now ask yourself how much of this vast treasure trove of resources is consumed rather than produced by students while they are in schools. It is a safe bet that while youth around the world are prolific in the extent to which they make creative contributions to the resources on the Internet, it is an equally safe bet that the vast majority of these contributions don't happen while they are in school. When students go from being passive consumers to active contributors to the Internet, not only will the world benefit from the vast untapped potential that is locked away in our young people, but we are also able to better prepare them for the creative and challenging lives and careers that they can successfully navigate and thrive in.

> When students go from being passive consumers to active contributors they are better prepared for creative and challenging lives and careers.

At its simplest definition, "create" means to develop something that didn't exist before. Being creative is not synonymous with the development of creative content for mass consumption. Creativity exists at many different levels of human endeavor. This applies equally to creative ways in which to order communities and societies or finding innovative solutions to many age-old problems that have dogged humanity. Creativity can exist on many different scales as well — from the smallest task that one does to having a vision to change the world.

Schools have an obligation to train students to be in touch with their creative side, and to help provide the "space," speaking both literally and metaphorically, where every student's creative skills will fully emerge. Ironically, the more "creative" a teacher is, the less likely that there will be a creative imperative for their students. That means, more open-ended problems that seem, on the face of it, to be "simple" and not creative often hold the greatest promise for students to exercise their own creative muscles. Of course this direction has other, important, ramifications. It implies that teachers are willing to give up much of their "control" in that they are prepared to accept learning and work products from students whose validity has not already been determined. We cover these areas under the "create" category:

- Music
- Performance
- Fine Arts
- Cooking and baking
- Technology-assisted media
- Writing

> Schools have an obligation to train students to be in touch with their creative side, and to help provide the "space," speaking both literally and metaphorically, where every student's creative skills will fully emerge.

6 CHAPTER CREATE

Figure 6-1, 6-2: *Music enhances listening, concentration, the development of small and large motor skills and coordination of senses like seeing, hearing and touch. Schools should make every effort to provide adequate facilities for both choral and instrumental music. This picture from March 2017 shows the Des Moines All-City Music Festival in which 400 middle school students participated. The orchestra, band and choir presented a concert at the Iowa State Fairgrounds.*
Photo © Phil Roeder.

- Making and building things
- Designing the learning environment

Music

From a learning standpoint, there is much more to music than singing or playing an instrument. Music enhances listening, concentration, the development of small and large motor skills and coordination of senses like seeing, hearing and touch. These are skills that will benefit students in many other aspects of their lives. There is evidence that music helps in many

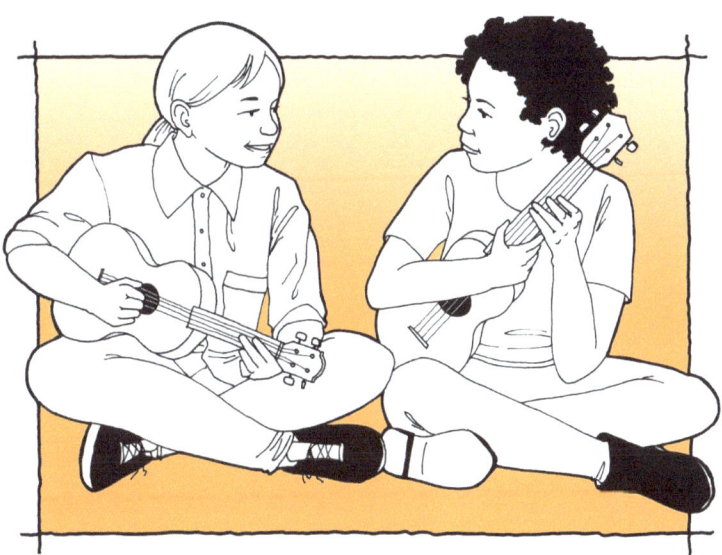

71

areas such as:[42]

Language Development: Exposure to music helps students strengthen their natural ability to decode sounds and words

Increased IQ: Research shows modest improvements in IQ in students who are exposed to music at an early age

> Music enhances listening, concentration, the development of small and large motor skills and coordination of senses like seeing, hearing, and touch.

Brain Works Harder: There is scientific evidence that students who regularly practice music show a larger growth of neural activity

Spatial-Temporal Skills: Musical activity improves spatial skills and improves a student's ability to succeed in subjects such as architecture, engineering, math, art, gaming, and especially working with computers

Being Musical: This is about giving students the gift of music for its own sake. Exposing students to music and music education from an early age will allow them to appreciate the beauty of music and make it a part of their aesthetic, cultural, and spiritual development.

There are a host of additional benefits of music education that are worth noting. These include:[43]

- Better memory
- Improved hand-eye coordination
- More engaged in school
- Success in society
- Emotional development
- Pattern recognition skills
- Builds imagination and curiosity
- Relaxing
- Builds discipline
- Teamwork
- Self-confidence

There are many ways in which students can be exposed to, participate in and be formally trained in music. Unlike some of the other activities that can be conducted in generic spaces, much of the formal learning in music needs spaces that are specially designed for this purpose. From individual and ensemble music practice rooms to choral and

> Once the fundamentals of music are mastered, it is also a subject in which creativity and originality can occur very naturally.

---

[42] The Benefits of Music Education By Laura Lewis Brown. PBS Parents. http://www.pbs.org/parents/education/music-arts/the-benefits-of-music-education/
[43] 20 Important Benefits of Music in Our Schools. National Association for Music Education https://nafme.org/20-important-benefits-of-music-in-our-schools/#comments

6 CHAPTER CREATE

Figure 6-3, 6-4: *The performing arts in school provide a rich template for creative expression. Many schools committed to giving students the best training possible in music and the performing arts are opting to develop black box theaters instead of or in addition to the regular school auditorium. The black box theater is a versatile space that provides ample opportunities for change and can be used for drama, dance, music, as a theater-in-the-round, media productions and as a multi-purpose presentation space. Black box theater at American School of Bombay.*

instrumental music studios, recording studios, black box theaters and auditoriums, there are a wide range of places within a school in which music can happen.

In this book, we have talked about the value of "experiences" over rote learning for its own sake. Music, like the other performing arts described here, is an area of study that naturally lends itself to being an experience. Once the fundamentals of music are mastered, it is also a subject in which creativity and originality can occur very naturally.

Performance

Just like with music, the performing arts in school provide a rich template for creative expression. This is an arena where students can shine and thrive who may not otherwise do well within the regimented framework of the traditional school day. In our research

73

on the subject of the benefits of the performing arts in school, we came across this great list compiled by the Bishop Tyrell Anglican College in Wallsend, Australia:[44]

> The performing arts in school provide a rich template for creative expression. This is an arena where students can shine and thrive who may not otherwise do well within the regimented framework of the traditional school day.

1. **Life Skills:** Students gain important life skills as they learn the value of critical feedback

2. **Creative Expression:** Through creative expression, students learn to comprehend our world better

3. **Better Prepared:** Students are better equipped to navigate the challenges they might be faced with upon graduating from secondary schooling

4. **Cognitive Abilities:** Drama and the performing arts allow an avenue to develop cognitive abilities that complement study in other disciplines. For example, drama students learn to approach situations in an array of different manners that can help to develop creative thinking and new study techniques

5. **Confidence and Public Speaking Skills:** It builds confidence, which benefits public speaking opportunities. The talent that students discover through the arts can form habits which transcend all areas of study

6. **Communication:** Communication between peers is accelerated as students are exposed to group activities. This experience also provides opportunity for students to display cultural leadership qualities.

Figure 6-5: *Sufficient data exists to overwhelmingly support the belief that study and participation in the fine arts is a key component in improving learning throughout all academic areas. The design and location of the art room deserves special attention. Good daylighting is an essential component. A space that feels more like an art "studio" as opposed to a classroom will help bring out the creative best in students. If possible, having an adjacent art terrace is a nice feature to have.*
Art Room at Leysin American School, Switzerland.

7. **Unique Voice:** Some students find their "voice" while studying the arts. They may discover they are natural problem solvers or leaders. Creative expression is a great way to build self-confidence and can be particularly beneficial for introverted and reserved children.

8. **Solitude toward Self-Discovery:** The Arts can also be a source of solitude – a place where a child is able to shut out their surrounds and immerse themselves in a creative environment. This process

Australia

Figure 6-6: *Art rooms for elementary schools also need to be "artistic" and studio-like. They need to look and feel different than a typical classroom. A little mixing and matching of the arts is also fine as we can see from the piano and guitar in this art room.*
Art Room at American School of Bombay.

allows the imagination to thrive, aiding internal exploration. It's a natural precursor to a well-developed sense of self.

9. **Emotional Intelligence and Independence:** The arts can act as an agent through which a variety of emotions can be learned, rehearsed and practiced. Adolescents can find it difficult to express their emotions and so the arts provides a great outlet for children to explore a wide range of feelings, including delight, anger, and unhappiness. This experience can define a child's growing sense of independence and interdependence.

This list shows that the performing arts, which used to be marginalized because of the perception that they did not provide the kind of "real" education found in math and science, actually provide very tangible, necessary and holistic skills that are closely aligned with the skills and talents that are essential for success now and in the years ahead.

> The fine arts also provide learners with non-academic benefits such as promoting self-esteem, motivation, aesthetic awareness, cultural exposure, creativity, improved emotional expression, as well as social harmony and appreciation of diversity.

Fine Arts

Fine arts fall into the same category as music and the performing arts in that they are, intrinsically, creative mediums in which students can express their uniqueness and originality.

"Sufficient data exists to overwhelmingly support the belief that study and participation in the fine arts is a key component in improving learning throughout all academic areas. Evidence of its effectiveness in reducing student dropout, raising student attendance, developing better team players, fostering a love for learning, improving greater student dignity, enhancing student creativity, and producing a more prepared citizen for the workplace for tomorrow can be found documented in studies held in many varied settings, from school campuses, to corporate America.

The fine arts also provide learners with non-academic benefits such as promoting self-esteem, motivation, aesthetic awareness, cultural exposure, creativity, improved emotional expression, as well as social harmony and appreciation of diversity."[45]

In the arena of school design, fine arts offers an excellent opportunity for school designers to provide ample opportunities for students of all ages to actively participate in art activities from drawing and painting to sculpture and craft-making. We believe that it is a lost opportunity for spaces that celebrate art not to themselves be artistically laid out with proper furnishings, good daylighting, and an aesthetically pleasing layout.

Cooking and Baking

Cooking and baking are inherently creative activities. Of course, not everyone who learns to cook or bake in school will end up as a professional chef, but these are essential skills that will be helpful throughout a student's life. When children don't have access to a healthy cooked meal they tend to eat highly processed foods heavy in fats and sugars. That is why learning to cook or bake is not just about making food but building awareness of health and nutrition and, by extension, learning to live a healthy life.

Extension.org provides the following compelling list of reasons that describe why it is important to cook in schools and at home with kids:[46]

1. Children may try new and healthy foods. Recent research published in the Journal of the Academy of Nutrition and Dietetics indicates that children engaged in tactile experiences, such as handling foods, have less food neophobia (food fear) and greater acceptance of eating a variety of foods.

2. A kitchen is a learning lab for children that can involve all of their senses. While kneading, tossing, pouring, smelling, cutting, and feeling foods, they have fun and learn without being aware of it.

---

[45] The importance of Fine Arts Education. KATY Independent School District. Compiled by Bob Bryant
http://www.katyisd.org/dept/finearts/Pages/The-Importance-of-Fine-Arts-Education-.aspx
[46] Cooking with Kids in Schools -- Why it is Important. Feb 2017. Extension.org.
http://articles.extension.org/pages/73371/cooking-with-kids-in-schools:-why-it-is-important

Figure 6-7: *Cooking and baking are inherently creative activities. Of course, not everyone who learns to cook or bake in school will end up as a professional chef, but these are essential skills that will be helpful throughout a student's life. Rather than the typical culinary arts lab based on a domestic kitchen model that schools tend to have, it is far more effective to have students working as chef interns in the school's professional kitchen and have a direct hand in preparing meals for student lunches and community events. Photo © Valencia College.*

3. Children who cook at home indicate a *"sense of accomplishment,"* self-confidence, and feeling of contributing to their families.

4. They spend time cooking instead of engaged in screen time.

5. Children tend to skip less healthy prepared or processed snack foods as they prepare their own food more.

6. Recent research indicates that nutrition knowledge may be incomplete without the experiential learning or hands-on activities associated with food preparation that involves handling food and cooking equipment.

7. Children learn lifetime skills through practicing basic math skills such as counting, weighing, measuring, and tracking time; they also gain social skills by working together and communicating in the kitchen.

8. Teaching cooking to youth is an opportunity to teach nutrition education such as planning

> When children don't have access to a healthy cooked meal, they tend to eat highly processed foods heavy in fats and sugars.

6 CHAPTER CREATE

Figure 6-8: Computers can assist in extending the creative potential of every artistic endeavor from photography and painting to sculpture and craft-making. Every type of traditional art has its own digital counterpart. Schools should provide access to digital art studios to students who are interested in exploring this fascinating nexus between technology and art. The curriculum itself can be somewhat open-ended so that the vast and largely untapped potential of these new mediums can be creatively explored. Photo © Irina Miroshnikova. https://www.flickr.com/photos/irishishka/

meals and making smarter food choices.

9. Cooking can aid children in acceptance of responsibility. Each child has a task to complete to contribute to the meal preparation and cleanup.

10. Cooking in schools can build positive memories that promote future healthy, enjoyable cooking elsewhere.

11. Children ate more fruits and vegetables after participating in culinary classes according to some research studies.

12. Many research studies show improved changes in cooking knowledge, food safety behaviors, and cooking self-efficacy.

13. Other studies indicate that teaching nutrition education with food preparation in science class is more effective than in nutrition education science classes without food preparation.

Most schools in the United States and around the world have full cooking kitchens that prepare and serve food to students. We recommend that anytime a kitchen is renovated or modernized,

> Computers can assist in extending the creative potential of every artistic endeavor from photography and painting to sculpture and craft-making.

every effort is made to convert it into a "teaching kitchen" so that students can learn how to cook in the authentic setting of a commercial kitchen as opposed to the "culinary labs" and "home economics labs" that contain a series of domestic cooking appliances. In Chapter 10, we have shown the design of a student-run cafeteria and kitchen called the "Young Chef's Studio." Whenever possible, foods prepared either wholly by students or with adult help should be for consumption so that "cooking class" doesn't feel like another theoretical exercise.

> Technology-assisted media changes the equation of creativity in schools. For example, we know that digital technologies are making it easier for kids to make art that they can publish and share.

Technology-Assisted Media

There are few domains in life that have not been affected by technology. In schools also, technology presents an opportunity and a challenge. It is an opportunity in that technology, via the Internet, connects students with a much wider array of expertise, information, and learning resources than they would have within the school itself. In the world of artistic endeavors, it also presents a challenge because it can extend the means of artistic expression far beyond traditional ways. For example, music can now be made and played on small electronic tablets in ways that look nothing like learning to play or compose music on traditional instruments like the piano or violin. Computers can assist in extending the creative potential of every artistic endeavor from photography and painting to sculpture and craft-making. That doesn't mean these art forms cannot exist in schools as they used to look in the pre-computer era. At the time of this writing there is still as much scope in life as there is in school for the "purer" forms of art to co-exist with the new media.

We have already discussed the more traditional art forms earlier in this chapter so let us look at how technology assisted media changes the equation of creativity in schools. For example, we know that, "Digital technologies are making it easier for kids to make art that they can publish and share."[47]

"In Pittsburgh, artists and educators, like those from Pittsburgh Filmmakers, are using digital technologies to help reimagine arts education and make it more participatory."

'We're using film to engage teens in critical thinking and to let them explore a more tangible form of science and art," said Pittsburgh Filmmaker mentor Marie Mashyna. The classes rely on a number of digital tools and emphasize the relationship between technology and art. "Learning about film helps them understand the current digital world more," Mashyna said in a recent blog post about the project.[48]

In her Masters Thesis Report at Western Michigan University titled, "Emerging Technologies in Art Education," Molly A. Marshall notes, "There are many examples of successful artists who collaborate. One example of this type of collaboration is through a website called the sketchbook project (www.sketchbookproject.com). By visiting this site, artist are able to find other artists to work with to create

> For the foreseeable future at least, writers who create original content remain insulated from the Artificial Intelligence wave that threatens to engulf many previously "safe" professions.

---

[47] How Technology is Moving Arts Education Beyond the Classroom. Remake Learning.
https://remakelearning.org/blog/2013/08/21/how-technology-is-moving-arts-education-beyond-the-classroom/
[48] Ibid

6 CHAPTER CREATE

Figure 6-9: *There are few creative activities that have stood the test of time as well as writing. As with any creative activity, writing will improve if students are allowed to get into flow. Comfortable seating at the proper height in a cheerful daylit and quiet space provide ideal conditions for writing regardless of whether the writing is being done on a computer or on paper.*

art."[49] Marshall goes on to cite S.E.K. Smith, who had this interesting observation about how technology is fostering a new kind of collaboration in art: "Collaborative methods of practice are increasingly the norm in contemporary art. Such works prioritize process over object production and technical proficiency, as well as social engagement and community over artistic autonomy. At the same time, the spheres of contemporary art and activism are increasingly intertwined."[50]

From a space design perspective, the proliferation of technology-assisted media in schools will require architects to engage more closely with students, artists and technology specialists to create environments that support the new technologies in both traditional and contemporary learning spaces. From specifying furniture that allows students to work comfortably with laptops to having more specialized places like black box theaters and recording studios, a new generation of school designers need to think about schools as places where suitable technologies are seamlessly integrated into the learning environment.

Writing

There are few creative activities that have stood the test of time as well as writing. For the foreseeable future at least, writers who create original content remain insulated from the Artificial Intelligence wave that threatens to engulf many previously "safe" professions and pursuits. Schools have always been big on writing but the manner in which it is structured and forced upon students robs it of both spontaneity and creativity. The classroom environments in which most student writing assignments happen are also not conducive to being creative. Libraries tend to be better for this purpose but the highly structured school schedule means that students are there for limited periods of time working on tight deadlines — again, factors that stifle creativity.

Literacy Professor Gail Tompkins provides this list of seven reasons why creative writing is important in schools:[51]

1. Entertain
2. Foster artistic expression

---

[49] Emerging Technologies in Art Education Molly A. Marshall, Masters Thesis, Western Michigan University https://scholarworks.wmich.edu/cgi/viewcontent.cgi?referer=https://www.bing.com/&httpsredir=1&article=1539&context=masters_theses
[50] Ibid. citation in Molly A. Marshall Thesis. Smith, S.E.K. (November 1, 2012). Working in the Space Between: Understanding Collaboration in Contemporary Artistic Practice. Reviews in Cultural Theory, volume 3. Retrieved from http://www.reviewsinculture.com/?r=97
[51] E. Tompkins, Gail. (1982). Seven Reasons Why Children Should Write Stories. Language Arts.

Figure 6-10: *Sylvia Martinez and Gary Stager write in Invent to Learn, a book that some call the "Maker in Education bible": "Maker classrooms are active classrooms. In active classrooms one will find engaged students, often working on multiple projects simultaneously, and teachers unafraid of relinquishing their authoritarian role. The best way to activate your classroom is for your classroom to make something." Maker Lab at Hillel School of Detroit, Michigan.*

3. Explore the functions and values of writing
4. Stimulate imagination
5. Clarify thinking
6. Search for identity
7. Learn to read and write

Robyn Ewing AM, vice president of Sydney Story Factory and professor of teacher education and the arts, notes that strong creative thinking and learning skills are critical to students' social and emotional well-being, academic achievement, and lifelong learning.[52]

So while there is a very strong case for the benefits of creative writing, it is our contention that there isn't a corresponding effort to encourage it in schools and, even when such efforts are made sincerely, the milieu in which children are asked to engage in writing doesn't foster the calm state of flow that is so essential for creative activities. Of course we also know that not everyone will be creative in the same kind of space. Some students want a quiet peaceful corner and others prefer the energy of a more casual and active space (think Starbucks) to get their creative juices

The shift to 'making' represents the perfect storm of new technological materials, expanded opportunities, learning through firsthand experience, and the basic human impulse to create.
-- *Gary Stager*

---

[52] Creative writing boosts kids' confidence and creativity. Oct. 2015. The University of Sydney
https://sydney.edu.au/news-opinion/news/2015/10/20/creative-writing-boosts-kids-confidence-and-creativity.html

Figure 6-11: *Creativity in the curriculum needs to be matched by dynamic and creative design of the learning environment. This high school entry space at the International School of Brussels can accommodate a full-school presentation or a small performance. When it is not used for large assemblies, the large steps become a social gathering area or a place for small group meetings and individual study.*

flowing. That is why we advocate a variety of both formal and informal settings that students can naturally occupy regardless of whether they are writing with pen and paper or using an electronic device like a computer, tablet, or even a phone.

Making and Building Things

When everything is said and done, there is no better way to express one's creativity than by making and building things. Unfortunately, most hands-on activities in schools have been circumscribed by their subject area and tend to be focused on science and art. Beyond these subjects, when students are working with their hands it is usually in an after-school program or a club. Of course, there has been the industrial arts and design technology courses, but these tended to be offered mostly to older students. Only recently, with the growth of the "maker movement" in schools that corresponds to the DIY movement outside school, are students of all ages getting the opportunity to design and build their own creations using a variety of modern tools like 3D printers, CNC routers and laser cutters. This trend has also taken off in the proliferation of STEM and STEAM curriculums, which are offered either as elective programs within existing schools or designed from the ground up as the theme around which entire new schools are being developed.

"Sylvia Martinez and Gary Stager write in Invent to Learn, a book that some call the 'Maker in Education bible': 'Maker classrooms are active classrooms. In active classrooms one will find engaged students, often working on multiple projects simultaneously, and teachers unafraid of relinquishing their authoritarian role. The best way to activate your classroom is for your classroom to make something.'"[53]

According to Gary Stager, "The shift to 'making' represents the perfect storm of new technological materials, expanded opportunities, learning through firsthand experience, and the basic human impulse to create. It offers the potential to make classrooms more child-centered: relevant and more sensitive to each child's remarkable capacity for intensity. Making is predicated on the desire that we all have to exert agency over our lives, to solve our own problems. It recognizes that knowledge is a consequence of experience, and it seeks to democratize access to a vast range of experience and expertise so that each child can engage in authentic problem solving."[54]

> When everything is said and done, there is no better way to express one's creativity than by making and building things.

For all the excitement generated by the Maker Movement, it is only now, and very slowly, making inroads into the school design arena. Most schools still talk about how to make "in the classroom" even though, as a space primarily designed for frontal instruction, the classroom is probably the worst place in school for making things due primarily to its limited space. We believe that making and doing should be such an intrinsic part of what children do in schools that "maker labs" should go the way of "computer labs" because every part of school should, in one way or the other, be able to support and facilitate the act of "making" — transforming an idea into a product. This will transform theory into practice in ways that makes learning (and, yes, even school) fun again.

---

[53] How the Maker Movement Is Moving Into Classrooms By Vicki Davis, Edutopia 2014
https://www.edutopia.org/blog/maker-movement-moving-into-classrooms-vicki-davis
[54] What's the Maker Movement and Why Should I Care? By Gary Stager. Scholastic. http://www.scholastic.com/browse/article.jsp?id=3758336

CHAPTER 7
HOW TO TRANSFORM

Figure 7-1: *When done well, schools will help students grow into balanced, happy and productive citizens each fulfilled according to his or her own potential. That requires getting students away from a one-size-fits all model of education represented by the classroom and into spaces like this temporary high school at the International School of Brussels.*

Change is not easy. This is especially true in the world of education, which has seen dozens of fads come and go over the past few decades. Compounding the problem is the fact that, in education, the "measures" of true success are elusive. When done well, schools will help students grow into balanced, happy, and productive citizens each fulfilled according to his or her own potential. This is a long-term goal, and all the "right" actions taken by schools to ensure these outcomes may not show short-term positive outcomes against the measures that schools put in place such as test scores and completed homework assignments. Author Michael Edwards asks, "Should education be evaluated using test scores or the skills we need to live well together?"[55]

Insofar as innovations in the arena of school facilities go, there are, unfortunately, not too many to speak of. With the fundamental foundation of school -- the classroom -- as a sacrosanct non-negotiable, architects are forced to express their innovations in the margins and in areas where they are given some creative freedom. That is why in the vast majority of school design awards, the photographs publicizing the school will be of the library or the entry atrium or the exterior elevations or even some common and breakout areas. The classrooms themselves, which remain the primary place where students spend most of their school day, rarely get featured other than to show off some new furniture.

There is a reason for the lack of enthusiasm to alter the familiar classroom-based model of school. It goes back to the first and only real large-scale attempt to define a new model of schooling in which the classroom does not have primacy. This attempt resulted in what we now know as the failed "open classroom" schools.

> When done well, schools will help students grow into balanced, happy, and productive citizens each fulfilled according to his or her own potential.

---

[55] Valuing What We Can Measure or Measuring What We Value? Michael Edwards. February 06, 2012 PHILANTOPIC Philanthrophy News Digest http://pndblog.typepad.com/pndblog/2012/02/valuing-what-we-can-measure-or-measuring-what-we-value.html

7 CHAPTER HOW TO TRANSFORM

Figure 7-2: *Just because students are not surrounded by the four walls of a classroom and are actively being "managed" by a teacher doesn't mean learning stops. Given a variety of spaces to learn in, students will naturally gravitate to the ones that work best for them. This kind of space design is vastly different from the open classroom schools in which there was little variety of space and, more important, there was no difference in pedagogy which continued to be teacher directed.*
PK Yonge Developmental Research School at the University of Florida, Gainesville.

Though well-intentioned and informed of the same misgivings about classrooms that this and other books discuss, the open-classroom movement had some fatal flaws that ensured its demise. First, there is the "someone forgot to tell the teachers" argument. Though the new designs put groups of 100 students or more in large open areas, teachers converted these spaces to makeshift "classrooms" using furnishings like file cabinets, desks and makeshift partitions and continued the teacher-directed instructional model that the spaces were never designed to accommodate. Second, the late 60's and early 70's was a time when the United States was in rebellion against the "experimental" culture that these kinds of schools seemed to embody. The third, and less understood reason, for the demise of the open classroom movement is that these were really poor from a design standpoint. Practically, it was a nightmare to "manage" 100 or more students in large open areas with poor

> Though well-intentioned and informed by the same misgivings about classrooms that this and other books discuss, the open-classroom movement had some fatal flaws that ensured its demise.

7 CHAPTER HOW TO TRANSFORM

Figure 7-3: *The factory model school was never a good solution. Children are not widgets and shouldn't be subject to processes designed to produce uniform products. The challenge with a more personal approach is that it goes counter to the classroom-based physical design of schools. That is why the proper design of learning environments is critical to ensure that each student has some choice and autonomy as to what, how and where he or she learns.*
American School of Bombay.

acoustics, very little variety in furnishings, and lack of variety of spaces that would be suitable for different modalities of learning. In this sense they ended up being exactly what they were rebelling against, very large classrooms with too many students.

"Without 'quiet zones,' restorative areas, enclosed spaces for smaller groupings and focused work, hand-picked furniture and acoustic treatments that would be essential for the different activity zones to work as desired, the open classroom design is almost certain to fail. Looking back at the actual design of the open classroom schools, it is evident that none of the above elements of design were actually put into place and so it is not surprising that open classroom schools were dismissed as a fad.

While open classroom schools stopped being built over 35 years ago they remain disproportionately influential today in decisions made about school design. Their legacy lives on mostly in the form of the myth that any change from a traditional classroom-based model of education represents a return to the failed open classroom movement."[56]

It is important to understand that there are two schools of thought about what represents a "good" education. One is presented by the conservatives, who believe that schools are fine

> Children are not widgets and shouldn't be subject to processes designed to produce uniform products.

---

[56] Introduction. Blueprint for Tomorrow: Redesigning Schools for Student-Centered Learning by Prakash Nair. Harvard Education Press. 2014

7 CHAPTER HOW TO TRANSFORM

Figure 7-4: *Norma Rose Point School in Vancouver, Canada is a publicly funded government school. It is an example of a project that was built from the ground up as a learning community school as opposed to a classroom based school. While this required a substantial shift in teachers' instructional practice, especially as it relates to collaboration with their peers, the school has had great success with its student-centered model of education. While the largest share of the credit goes to the school leadership and teachers, it is the building project that allowed Norma Rose Point to be the exemplar of excellence it is today.*

as they are, have served society nobly for over a hundred years, and need no substantial change. This group would be horrified by any attempt to move away from classroom-based education and tend to dismiss such moves as misguided. To them, the open classroom movement was a fad that proved their thesis right.

The other school of thought, the one we belong to, believes that the factory model school was never a good solution. Children are not widgets and shouldn't be subject to processes designed to produce uniform products. There is the dehumanizing element of standardization and then there is the practical challenge of creating a system that will actually help all students realize

> Today, small businesses, big corporations, and even several higher education institutions have started to demand that students graduating from schools do so with a different skill set than they may have accepted a few years ago.

their full potential by giving them the necessary skills to navigate an increasingly complex world.

The progressive vision for a more personal approach to education, one that is focused on developing relevant skills for the world and jobs of tomorrow, has been gathering steam for the past couple of decades. Today, small businesses, big corporations, and even several higher education institutions have started to demand that students graduating from schools do so with a different skill set than they may have accepted a few years ago.

> Changes, especially systemic ones, don't happen spontaneously. They need a trigger or a catalyst.

Individual schools and even large school districts are now waking up to this new reality and are looking for ways to reinvent themselves. Unlike the fads that characterize previous reform initiatives, the changes that are now happening are at a structural level and are here to stay. Slowly, those who have decided to become the pioneers of the latest reform movement towards a more humane, equitable, and student-centered model of education are shifting the thinking of the entire education establishment. Wholesale reform may still be years away but big changes are already underway.

In the rest of this chapter, we will discuss the steps that schools and school districts can take when they are ready to take the Bold Moves (to quote Heidi Hayes Jacobs) needed to transform themselves to become relevant again.

Capital Spending as the Catalyst for Change

Changes, especially systemic ones, don't happen spontaneously. They need a trigger or a catalyst. In this book, we focus on school construction expenditures as the catalyst for change. That doesn't mean schools cannot change without construction money, but the kind of holistic changes that we are discussing are more likely to happen when both the "hardware" (the learning environment) and the "software" of education move synchronistically and in tandem.

Regardless of where a particular institution may be in its own journey, all those who embark on transformation must ask and answer two questions.

1. Why us and why now?
2. How do we go about this?

The precise answers to these two questions will vary quite a bit from school to school and from school organization to school organization, but here are some generic responses to the questions that we suggest. If you are a school organization contemplating change, and particularly if you are seeking to leverage your school construction funds as a catalyst to bring about the change, then some of these may be relevant to you — modified as needed to suit your specific situation, of course.

> What used to be our strength, the classical education we deliver, could also be our downfall in that we may be offering a product that becomes less and less relevant over time.

Figure 7-5: *Seventh Grade German Language Class at International School of Düsseldorf (ISD) utilizes the flexible space in the Senior School Innovation Lab (a newly renovated space) for a quick review discussion before transforming the space for a skit. ISD is a highly reputed private international school but they recognize the imperative to keep their facilities updated and in sync with their innovative educational offerings. Photo by Isaac Williams.*

Why Us and Why Now?

Many different kinds of schools will be looking for an opportunity to use their capital construction program as an opportunity to make broader changes to their educational model. Here are some examples of the different kinds of schools who, when faced with having to spend money on their school facilities, will answer the above "Why Us and Why Now" question differently but notice how each group sees capital construction as a significant milestone that, by its very rarity and longevity, provides an incentive for those in charge to think like futurists:

1. **Private Local/International School:** We are a successful private school and have established a solid reputation for excellence over many years. What used to be our strength, the classical education we deliver, could also be our downfall in that we may be offering a product that becomes less and less relevant over time. Reputation alone will not be enough for discerning parents who want to give their children the best of what contemporary education has to offer. The time is right now to think about transformation while we still hold a position as an industry leader. This is what leaders are expected to do; not just sit on our laurels but embrace the future and keep forging ahead. On the flip side, by not acting

> Our educational model that is focused heavily on academics is failing our students in that we are not equipping them adequately with soft skills.

Figure 7-6: *Students who come from difficult personal circumstances need to see relevance in what they are learning to improving their own lives. The High School for Recording Arts provides students the opportunity to achieve a high school diploma through the exploration and operation of the music business and other creative endeavors.*

Architect: Fielding Nair International. Randall Fielding worked closely with David Ellis, HSRA Founder, to realize their vision by creating a unique "Live, Play, Engage, and Create" environment that allows for a personalized, student-centered and hands-on learning experience.

now, we will be forced into change to keep pace with competitors or simply slide into irrelevance as our offerings become less and less attractive to the highly selective audience we cater to.

2. **Inner City School in an Underserved Community:** We are an inner city school that has struggled to keep pace academically with other, better positioned schools that have access to students from higher socio-economic groups and more qualified teachers. The old ways no longer serve our students. They do not have the aptitude, the interest, or the patience to sit for hours on end absorbing what, to them, seem like useless facts having no relevance to their daily existence which is, mostly, a struggle. For our children, school needs to be a place that offers more than just a series of meaningless "classes." They need to see relevance in what they are learning to improving their own lives and they need to get excited and proactively engage with what is happening in school. They need to be in a school that meets their academic, social, mental, physical, emotional, and spiritual needs. Try as we might, and stuck as we are in a system that is blind to the special and individual needs of our children, we believe the time is right for us to break free and do something bold and different.

7 CHAPTER HOW TO TRANSFORM

3. **Reputed Public School:** We are a public school and, by all measures, our students are doing well. Our facilities are not new but reasonably well maintained. We expect to see some modest growth in enrollment over the next few years. We are planning a substantial capital improvement project to upgrade our school buildings and grounds. The school district has a well-established facilities department and they have school building standards that are kept updated. They are prepared to hire a good local architect on our behalf who is highly experienced in the design of public schools. However, everything we have studied about the future of education confirms what we have known now for a few years. Our educational model that is focused heavily on academics is failing our students in that we are not equipping them adequately with soft skills like complex problem solving, critical thinking, creativity, and other skills identified by the World Economic Forum that they will need to be successful in college and in life. Therefore, we would like to direct the capital funds that are earmarked for our school towards the development of an innovative campus that reflects what a new vision for education for today and tomorrow should look like. In doing so, we wish to put aside all the school building "standards" our district has developed and use the funds as we see fit utilizing renowned education and design professionals to guide our thinking as we move down this new path. Obviously, we need to do this now because this is when the construction funds are available and, once spent, we will no longer have this golden opportunity to reinvent ourselves.

> There was no miracle moment. Instead, a down-to-earth, pragmatic, committed-to-excellence process kept each company, its leaders, and its people on track.

4. **Highly Regarded Public School District:** We are a successful public school district with increasing enrollment and some of our school buildings need to be upgraded and some need to be replaced. We also have the need for one new elementary school to be constructed in a new neighborhood. We are confident that our community will approve a bond referendum to fund our district's capital needs program. We see this as a golden opportunity to serve our students by directing our capital funds toward the design of new and renovated facilities that reflect a new educational paradigm more in keeping with tomorrow's needs than the buildings in which our schools are currently housed. Everything we have researched about education tells us that we need to do better for our students. We believe that our school buildings are the best and most visible evidence of what we believe education should look like. Currently, there is a big disconnect between our aspirations as a community to offer the best, personalized learning experiences for our students and what we are actually offering to them. The building program that will be funded by the bond referendum is an ideal opportunity to bring our school district emphatically into the future.

5. **New Private School:** We are new to the world of education. We are in this to create a school, and possibly more if the first one succeeds, that is designed both educationally and architecturally from the ground up to meet today's and tomorrow's needs. We need our school to be driven not by preconceived notions of what a school is supposed to look like but by research from the world of education, neurology, and environmental design. We

> We need our school to be driven not by preconceived notions of what a school is supposed to look like but by research from the world of education.

91

Figure 7-7: By any measure, Bloomfield Hills would be considered one of the most affluent communities in Michigan. However, with their old high schools falling quickly into disrepair, the school district decided to build a new and consolidated Bloomfield Hills High School. The new high school dispensed altogether with the classroom model and chose, instead, to have all students study in Learning Communities. This image shows students managing their own learning in a small group room within a learning community. Photo © James Haefner.

7 CHAPTER HOW TO TRANSFORM

> " We want the new to reflect our heritage and our spiritual outlook while also providing the best that a contemporary education can provide.

would like to create a learning environment that is culturally appropriate, academically relevant, and based on hands-on, experiential learning. With the proliferation of factory model schools, children have few alternatives when it comes to getting a real, meaningful and relevant education. We hope our school will provide that and, in the process, inspire others who are contemplating the development or redesign of their schools to build for tomorrow and not for yesterday.

6. Reputable Parochial School: We are a parochial school and have a sterling reputation for delivering quality education. We are housed in an old historic building and want to tread carefully in making changes to our campus that preserves our cachet while upgrading our offerings. We are not looking for radical or revolutionary changes but we do realize that along with the changes to our facilities, we have a golden opportunity to also rethink our educational model so that our students will continue to have the best opportunities to succeed in college and in life. We want the new to reflect our heritage and our spiritual outlook while also providing the best that a contemporary education can provide.

Interestingly, the second question, "How do we go about this?" can be answered almost identically (except for group #5 above — a new entity and starting from scratch). So here is a way, in answering question two, where all these different educational groups find common ground.

HOW DO WE GO ABOUT THIS?

Step ONE: A Systematic Process with the Right People "On the Bus"

Jim Collins in his book, **Good to Great** said something that has proven itself time and time again when it comes to successful school transformations. In his words, "In each of these dramatic, remarkable, good-to-great corporate transformations, we found the same thing: There was no miracle moment. Instead, a down-to-earth, pragmatic, committed-to-excellence process—a framework—kept each company, its leaders, and its people on track for the long haul."[57]

---

[57] Good to Great: Why Some Companies Make the Leap...And Others Don't. By Jim Collins

7 CHAPTER HOW TO TRANSFORM

Figure 7-8: *Boulder Valley Schools (see chapter 9 for detailed case study) directed a substantial portion of its bond money for school construction into new schools like Creekside Elementary School pictured here whose spaces are configured to look nothing like most public schools in the country. These schools are optimized for high student achievement measured against the school district's own Innovative Guiding Principles.*

What Collins noted is found in the hybrid "stories" we have told above of the various groups seeking change. Hope and not fear should be the driver of change and a systematic process rather than a revolutionary upheaval is most likely to yield the desired results.

Collins also talked about a second important principle that is strongly applicable to the school transformation process where facilities spending is the catalyst for such change. This deals with the "who" and "where." Again, in Collins' own words, "Leaders of companies that go from good to great start not with 'where' but with 'who.' They start by getting the right people on the bus, the wrong people off the bus, and the right people in the right seats. And they stick with that discipline—first the people, then the direction—no matter how dire the circumstances."[58]

In the case of schools, we recommend that before any decisions are made regarding the nature or extent of the changes that will be made, an advisory group of highly experienced representative stakeholders be put together to direct the capital project and monitor its progress

> Schools impact property values, they can have a forceful iconic presence that defines the quality and character of the neighborhood in which they are located, and they can become symbols of civic stature and pride.

---

[58] Ibid

7 CHAPTER HOW TO TRANSFORM

Figure 7-9: *Few schools in the world have taken the message of personalization and student-centered learning to heart in the way VEGA school in New Delhi, India has done. See Chapter 10 case study. Here, there is a true melding of form and function. The learning spaces provide a great variety of opportunities for the democratic model of education practiced by VEGA.*

Figure 7-10: *Hillel School of Detroit has always had a sterling reputation for delivering a high quality education. However, they were stuck in a building where the classroom was the dominant academic element. Over the course of a few years, Hillel School completely transformed not only their facilities but, in the process, did a major update of both pedagogy and curriculum. Today, Hillel's reputation for excellence is reflected in the design of its innovative learning spaces that are facilitating the development of essential life and academic skills.*

Figure 7-11: *It is important for the Project Leadership Team to set the overall direction for the facilities project. This will provide the framework of schedule and budget within which the larger stakeholder community's input can be analyzed and a final scope of work determined. The first step (particularly for larger projects involving the rethinking of multiple buildings across a full campus) is the development of a Facilities Master Plan.*

Picture shows Facilities Master Plan Leadership Team meeting with Fielding Nair International led by the School Superintendent Dr. Chip Kimball at Singapore American School.

and effectiveness. We often refer to such a team as the PLT, which is short for "Project Leadership Team." The first task of the PLT is to bring on board a reputed firm with impeccable credentials that can be equally comfortable in the area of educational innovation as they are in the design of new-paradigm architectural solutions for educational institutions. With this core in-house/consultant team on board, you are ready for step two.

Step TWO — Discovery

The process of Discovery is exactly what it sounds like. This is where the PLT and the selected school architect/change agent meet with all the key school stakeholders utilizing a variety of strategies from visioning exercises, roundtable discussions, and lectures to hands-on workshops, site walks, and the examination of opportunities and constraints. During this process, school board members, the school leadership, representative groups of students and parents, the teachers at the school, school benefactors and sponsors and local community elders will all be consulted. It is during this phase that the leadership of the school will have to grapple with what Prof. Richard Elmore defines as their own "theory of learning." "In an ideal world, schools and the systems in which they are embedded would model for the rest of society what learning should look like. In the real world, schools often model what learning used to look like in a world that no longer exists."[59] While this may be true in fact and in practice, schools will rarely admit or even realize that they are moving rapidly towards irrelevance. By going through a

---

[59] Richard Elmore. Part Two of this book

7 CHAPTER HOW TO TRANSFORM

visioning exercise where they have to look honestly at their own systems and practices using Prof. Elmore's theories of learning as their framework, they will at least have to start with the reality of where they are and use that to close the gap to where they want to be aspirationally.

> " In an ideal world, schools and the systems in which they are embedded would model for the rest of society what learning should look like.

Schools are centers of community serving more than the students enrolled there. Schools also impact property values, they can have a forceful iconic presence that defines the quality and character of the neighborhood in which they are located, and they can become symbols of civic stature and pride. As such, school transformations will tend to attract a wider audience of interested stakeholders than changes by other institutions.

At the conclusion of the on-site Discovery meetings and workshops, a large amount of data will be collected that need to be sorted and analysed. This will lead to the development of several Guiding Principles for both education and the physical space design that will inform all the work to follow. The case-study chapter on Boulder Valley School District discusses this in greater depth.

Step THREE — Developing the Educational Ecosystem Document

Very early on in our practice as school architects, we realized that architecture, in and of itself, while it may represent a powerful and visible element of change, is not enough to bring about real, meaningful and sustainable change in the education itself. Delving deeper into what worked and what did not, we recognized that, like every other enterprise, a school is also a well-integrated "system." Even when the desired results are not being delivered it wasn't always because the system wasn't working but, in fact, because it *was* working as it was designed to — but in conflict with the changes we were seeking to implement.

Figure 7-12: *Teachers rank highly among the many key school stakeholder groups. Once they are convinced that they aren't losing classrooms but gaining a whole community of learning spaces, they become strong allies in the change process.*

Teachers at Col.legi Montserrat in Barcelona, Spain, suggesting ways in which their traditionally designed school building can be transformed into a modern learning environment.

Think about the various elements of a school's operations. They include:

1. School's vision and mission
2. Curriculum
3. Schedule
4. Learning Spaces
5. Teacher readiness
6. Parent expectations
7. Government regulations and standards
8. Assessments
9. Technology
10. Services — food, transportation, uniforms, etc.
11. Community resources

> Design is a much more collaborative process between the architect and the school than it has ever been before.

Each of the eleven elements noted above will have a series of subcomponents that define how it works at any given school.

The "Educational Ecosystem" that we refer to here is a Master Strategic Plan at the highest levels that looks at each of the above components of the system holistically as it currently exists and superimposes a new, aspirational map to determine what elements are in consonance with and what elements are in conflict with what exists today. So, for example, should the new vision call for a more experiential curriculum, it is possible that the existing schedule of 45 minute periods have to change along with various other elements such as how to measure student project quality, how to present the new model to parents, how to make sure teachers are adequately trained and so on.

The superimposition of the new over the old ecosystem will identify all the conflicts and "gaps" that need to be met under each of the above categories so that the whole "System" is in alignment and that no internal conflicts exist. While the above example lists 11 categories, some of them can be collapsed into others and schools can come up with their own version of their Educational Ecosystem. Once done, this document will become an effective way to monitor and manage change.

> What we are suggesting is that, when it comes to design, "Form Follows Vision."

Unlike the first three steps, the following steps are not necessarily done in sequential fashion. In fact, there is value in working on them concurrently because of their inter-relatedness and the manner in which work on one step may influence the decisions being made in one of the other steps.

Step FOUR — Implementing the Design

The change process we have described here has an interesting twist when it comes to design. The normal practice when it comes to architecture, and especially schools, is to follow the safe and established dictum, "Form Follows Function." We suggest ditching this motto for the simple reason that "form" and "function" are being designed concurrently and constantly informing

7 CHAPTER HOW TO TRANSFORM

A SAMPLE INTEGRATED EDUCATION ECOSYSTEM

Principles

1. Learning is founded in **inquiry**
2. Learning fosters a culture of **curiosity and risk taking**
3. **Mastery** of learning is demonstrated in multiple ways
4. Learning is a **social process**
5. Students solve **real problems** in their local or global community
6. Learning is **personalized and learner led**

Outcomes

1. **Thought Leaders** and **Pioneers in Advanced Technology**
2. **Self-directed Learners** and **Entrepreneurs**
3. **Stewards** of the Global Environment
4. Expert **Communicators** and **Storytellers**
5. **Attuned to people** and cultures around them

Methods

1. **Shared** teacher and student **leadership**
2. Regular, **cohesive unit planning**
3. **Multi-cohort** instruction
4. **Thematic** integrated projects and courses
5. **Personalized, technology enhanced** learning

Systems

1. **Cohesive** instructional goals
2. **Flexible** teaching arrangements
3. **Co-facilitated** cohort scheduling
4. **Need-based** instructional grouping (across cohort or subject)
5. **Multiple credit pathways**

Environment

1. **Fluidly connected** learning communities
2. **Varied** spaces supporting differentiation
3. Spaces for **collaborative, individual** and **active** learning
4. Connected to **nature**
5. Supports connection to **local & global community**

Assessment

1. **Formative AND summative**
2. **Continuous** and **data-driven**
3. **Student-constructed**
4. **Technology-supported**
5. **Teacher** and **peer-connected**
6. Student **self-assessment and reflection**

Figure 7-13: *As this graphic of a sample educational ecosystem shows, the learning environment is just one critical component of a larger "system" with many related components. School design can be most effective when it serves as the catalyst to reimagine the whole system rather than just as a way to improve learning spaces.*

Figure 7-14: *New 3D modeling techniques now allow clients to actually "see" the design emerging in near photorealistic form. In this rendering, the pattern of windows reflects the non-linear ratios found in nature and the overall sculptural form breaks the pattern of sameness in the region, where schools often appear the same as hotels and office buildings.*

Rendering of new secondary school for the Yew Chung International School of Chongqing by Fielding Nair International.

and influencing one another.

So, what we are suggesting is that, when it comes to design, "Form Follows Vision." The vision for what the school will be is the only "non-negotiable" and this will be expressed in the form of the "guiding principles" that we referred to earlier. This is applicable to both the design of the educational model as well as the architecture of the school.

Design is an inherently creative process and so having the education and physical designers work closely and in harmony is likely to yield innovative solutions that the traditional process (in which a program of spaces is handed to the architect) would never yield.

Another thing to keep in mind is that the technologies used in the world of architecture provide some previously unthinkable opportunities for school clients to actively participate in the development of the design as it progresses from a master plan and initial concepts into schematic design, design development, and construction documents. New 3D modeling techniques will allow clients to actually "see" the design emerging in near photorealistic form and taking shape through the issuance of the tender documents to the construction contractor. Elements such as lighting, colors, furnishings, floor, wall, and ceiling finish materials can all be viewed virtually before any final decisions are made in these areas.

Design is, therefore, a much more collaborative process between the architect and the school than it has ever been before. The added advantage of this is the reduced number of changes that will be needed during and after construction is completed.

Step FIVE — Implementing the Educational Initiatives

Design and vision have to inform each other and so even as the architects are exploring creative solutions there will be a "learning design" component that will start to get fleshed out. This is where the work done during Discovery and the examination of each school's Theory of Learning will come in handy. At the highest levels, the Discovery process will provide direction. This will be augmented by the work done during the process of creating the Educational Ecosystem described above. This step of the implementation process is about closing the gaps between what is there currently and what needs to be done to realize the school's educational vision.

This is where the real work of building a new curriculum, realigning schedules, choosing appropriate resources including technologies and educational partners and, most important, professional development to close teacher readiness gaps will happen. "Professional development is the strategy schools and school districts use to ensure that educators continue to strengthen their practice throughout their career. The most effective professional development engages teams of teachers to focus on the needs of their students. They learn and problem solve together in order to ensure all students achieve success."[60]

---

[60]Why Professional Development Matters by Hayes Mizell. Learning Forward 2010. LearningForward.org
https://learningforward.org/docs/default-source/pdf/why_pd_matters_web.pdf

Figure 7-15: *High quality learning spaces are just the beginning. It's effectiveness will depend on how well it inspires the important work of building a new curriculum, realigning schedules, choosing appropriate resources including technologies and educational partners and, most important, professional development designed to help teachers get the most out of their new or renovated spaces.*

Lauren Mehrbach, Learning Designer and Head of Middle School at Singapore American School, running a facilities-related PD workshop for teachers at American Embassy School in New Delhi, India.

It is the word "success" that gets exposed to the light of day during Discovery and the Creation of the Educational Ecosystem. Obviously, schools that have defined success as high test scores or college admissions will employ different professional development strategies than those that focus on the more holistic definition of success where every student leaves school with the important life skills discussed earlier in the heart of this book under the Live, Play, Engage and Create chapters.

> Excitement and fear are two sides of the same coin. Fear of change is a much more potent force in education than in other industries.

Step SIX — Aligning Governance, Management and Operations with the New Model

Many of the elements needed to successfully implement step five, Educational Initiatives, can only happen when the schools are suitably amended to align with the new vision. For example, a distributed leadership model where teachers are more empowered may require breaking down some of the traditional hierarchy in a school which has multiple layers of authority. Similarly, teachers may be given greater control and autonomy when it comes to the delivery of the curriculum and schedules may have to be realigned.

Some of the authority traditionally vested in the Board of Directors of the school or, in the case of public schools, controls exercised by the district leadership, may be redistributed or eliminated entirely. Principals may become more active in teaching as they are assisted by others in administrative matters. The school may enter into mutually beneficial partnerships with local community and business entities. In other words, the whole "system" under which any school operates will need to be aligned so that everyone is pulling in the right direction. This process is where the gaps identified by the Educational Ecosystem in the non-educational support areas are closed as new measures are implemented to give form to the new, transformed vision of the school.

Step SEVEN — Getting the Word Out

This is where concerted and coordinated communication efforts are made to win wide stakeholder support for the new direction the school has decided to go in. This is a vitally important step and, when done correctly, it has the potential to build consensus amongst the diverse stakeholders who control each school's destiny.

Excitement and fear are two sides of the same coin. Fear of change is a much more potent force in education than in other industries because the rewards, as previously noted, being long-term by nature, are not as readily apparent as one might expect given the "cost" of the change. Risk of failure is seen, and rightly so, as unacceptable because the lives of children are, literally, at stake.

If the thoughtful, methodical and tested processes described above are carefully followed, then there is, actually, no risk of failure. This statement has to be balanced by the very real fact that the greatest risk of failure facing most schools today is to look the other way and do nothing. This head-in-the-sand approach in the face of the sea changes occuring in the "learning realm" that used to be schools' mostly exclusive domain just a few decades ago poses a much greater threat to schools than walking down the path of change fully prepared and with the right strategies.

All this will be readily apparent to those who take the time to study the thorough change process the school has embarked on and described in this book. The authors are describing processes that have themselves tried, tested and adopted successfully

7 CHAPTER HOW TO TRANSFORM

Figure 7-16: *The elementary school at the American School of Bombay opened in the fall of 2012. This picture was taken during a visit to the school in 2017 by members of the Fielding Nair International team who served as the Design Architects for the school. The spaces in 2017 looked substantially different than they did in 2012 without any construction which is the hallmark of a "learning building."*

in New York liked to put it, "An educated consumer is our best customer."[61]

Step EIGHT — Keep it Going

It would be wonderful if we could tell you that once the above seven steps are completed, you are home free. That is, unfortunately, not the case! As with any enterprise, especially in today's rapidly evolving climate afflicting every single industry, educational transformations are also an ongoing, dynamic process. What we have defined is a framework within which the change itself never ceases. In fact, we advocate that even the buildings themselves (perhaps the one component of education that we most take for granted as "fixed") remain "alive" and coined the term "Learning Building" to signify this quality. Here is what we said in an earlier book on the subject: "We need to move away from the rigidity of the static building to the agility of the 'learning building.' The thesis of this book is that a well-designed school building will look very different day-to-day, week-to-week, month-to-month and year-to-year. The changes one observes will be a direct result of the school's occupants shaping their learning

> Be open and prepared for whatever new and exciting opportunities are around the next corner.

---

[61] Slogan used in television ads in the 1980s by Syms Corp (styled as SYMS), an off-price retail clothing store chain, founded by Sy Syms in 1959.

7 CHAPTER HOW TO TRANSFORM

Figure 7-17: *This is a photo of a groundbreaking ceremony in which the entire community, and especially children, participated. Community involvement and support is a key to the success of innovatively designed schools that will look and feel different than anything parents, teachers and students have seen before. Meadowlark School in Erie, Colorado for Boulder Valley School District.*

environment to fit the needs of the learning activity it needs to accommodate."[62]

The efficacy of the "learning building" was readily apparent in a recent visit we made to the elementary school campus of the American School of Bombay. We designed this school in early 2011 and it has been in operation ever since. What struck us was how different the school looked during our latest visit in 2017 compared to the way it had been organized when the school first opened. In fact, almost everything about the school looked different and, yet, we were informed that little to no capital dollars had been expended in making the changes to the organization of the school. All this was accomplished via the relocation of the many movable partitions that we had put in place and some new furnishings. By creating the "bones" of the original school to permit exactly these kinds of changes over time, we ensured that ideas that seemed current and relevant in 2011 would not forever trap the school into organizational models decades after the physical school had been constructed.

This same agility that we saw in the buildings was equally apparent in all aspects of the American School of Bombay. To them, change is not something to be afraid of but just a way of life, and they embrace it enthusiastically! We recommend this mindset for all schools embarking on the change journey. Be open and prepared for whatever new and exciting opportunities are around the next corner — and there are certain to be many if the last decade is any indication of where the future is headed.

---

[62] Introduction. Blueprint for Tomorrow: Redesigning Schools for Student-Centered Learning by Prakash Nair. Harvard Education Press. 2014

CHAPTER 8
PATHFINDERS — TAKING THE FIRST STEP

The saying "let's not bite off more than we can chew" is a mantra that we would advise all those interested in true and lasting education change to live by. Regardless of whether you are a 200-student school or have 4,000 students enrolled, and regardless of how strategic you have been lining up all your stakeholders behind a contemporary model of education, the actual process of change will still be difficult and complex. There will simply be too many moving parts and, in the end, when the plans are too ambitious, what we see, time and again, being rolled back are the innovations -- the very things the whole process was designed to encourage. To get around this problem, and for several years now, we recommend that schools start with small-scale, high-visibility projects. Ideally, this would be one or more learning communities of 100-150 students along with 4-6 teachers.

We call these small-scale pilot projects "Pathfinders" because they help each school find its own unique "path" to success. There are several advantages to starting the change journey with one or more Pathfinder projects. Among them:

Pathfinders can be built around what we label, "low-hanging fruit." Schools will choose to work on projects that can be accomplished with the least amount of effort. For example, this would involve the selection of spaces to renovate that pose the least amount of technical or structural challenges.

Teachers can "self-select." Since Pathfinders are small in scale, they do not need the buy-in from all the staff at the school. Schools will sometimes internally "advertise" the need for innovative teachers to work as an integral part of the selected Pathfinder team. Only those who volunteer will be considered. Schools may sweeten the pot for teachers brave enough to step up by giving them a special designation such as "Innovation Fellow"[63] and/or provide an additional financial incentive represented by a modest increase in salary. By limiting those working in the Pathfinders only to

Figure 8-1: *Horace Greeley High School in Chappaqua is a public school serving grades 9-12, and is one of the highest ranked high schools in the United States. Intent on continuing their record of excellence, the school developed this iLab that was converted out of three traditional classrooms as their first Pathfinder project. Its immense success has led to more innovative teaching and learning practices being adopted not only in the rest of the school but throughout the school district.*

---

[63] This was the case with the iLab — Innovation Lab at Horace Greeley High School in Chappaqua, New York

> **Since Pathfinders are small in scale, they do not need the buy-in from all the staff at the school.**

those who choose to serve voluntarily, there is a greater chance of success since there will be no "snipers" who are more interested in preserving the status quo. In our experience, Pathfinder projects so dramatically alter the education landscape that they stand apart as shining examples of what the future could look like. Juxtaposed, as they are, alongside the old model that is represented by the rest of the school, the quantitative and qualitative benefits of the new model represented by the Pathfinders become quickly apparent This method for ushering in change lets it happen spontaneously and is driven by inspiration rather than coercion. Schools and school districts that scale up change utilizing Pathfinders to blaze the way have a far greater chance of success than those that try to bring about wholesale cultural change within a school.

Figure 8-2: This Pathfinder space is an innovation lab at the Academy of the Holy Names in Tampa, Florida for middle school students. It used to be a traditional computer lab. The success of this Pathfinder led the school to create a similar space for the high school and extend this teaching and learning model across the whole middle school by means of a major renovation project.

8 CHAPTER PATHFINDERS — TAKING THE FIRST STEP

![kindergarten learning suite]

Figure 8-3: *Note the folding doors between two adjacent kindergarten studios. These used to be separate "classrooms" with individual teachers managing only their "own" students. Now, with the partition open (as it tends to be most of the time), SAS has created a "learning suite" where students and teachers mingle freely between the two studios. This arrangement also allows for sharing resources and creating a greater variety of learning experiences for students.*

Pathfinders have the greatest chance of success when they are distinguished by a set of design guiding principles that can be translated into action. For example, here are some guiding principles that an academic Learning Community Pathfinder may choose to exemplify in the space design, in the curriculum, in the scheduling of the day, in the pedagogy and the manner in which students and teachers are grouped.

1. Teachers shall not "own" rooms but will share a common workspace
2. Teachers shall work collaboratively to design and deliver an interdisciplinary curriculum
3. Lessons shall be planned in a manner that limits direct instruction while maximizing student autonomy, teamwork, and engagement
4. In completing their assignments, students will be exposed to multiple learning modalities and guided to use a variety of spaces that best meets their needs

Some examples of good Pathfinders that were successfully scaled up include:

Horace Greeley High School in Chappaqua, NY that started with an iLab (innovation lab) that later

> Pathfinders have the greatest chance of success when they are distinguished by a set of design guiding principles that can be translated into action.

8 CHAPTER PATHFINDERS — TAKING THE FIRST STEP

Figure 8-4: *Multiple modalities of learning can now happen simultaneously because of the larger "footprint" of the two rooms that allows teachers not to have to duplicate all the various "learning centers." Students can read quietly and independently as this child is doing with less distractions than in the older individual classroom spaces.*

morphed into various other projects at Horace Greeley and all the other schools in the District.

Academy of the Holy Names in Tampa, FL started with an iLab in their library and used this as a springboard to completely transform their entire Middle School.[64]

A successful Pathfinder is the work being done by the Middle School at Singapore American School. They practice the "Build it, Live it and Own it" philosophy. At the time that this book was being written, two of the SAS middle school educators wrote a compelling piece about how their new "Learning Community" model works. Their article is published here with permission exactly as it appeared in SAS' Teacher Perspectives Blog.[65]

Why Flexible Learning Environments?

> When the plans are too ambitious, what we see being rolled back are the innovations — the very things the whole process was designed to encourage.

---

[64] The transformation is about space, schedule, pedagogy and teacher collaboration.
[65] Why Flexible Learning Environments? Singapore American School, Perspectives Blog, Teacher Perspective by Lauren Mehrbach and Chris Beingessner, June 5, 2018

8 CHAPTER PATHFINDERS — TAKING THE FIRST STEP

By Lauren Mehrbach and Chris Beingessner

Last year, the SAS middle school worked with Fielding Nair International, an educational architecture firm, to renovate our sixth grade A-side team space to create a more flexible learning environment. This summer we are embarking on two more renovations, to 6B and 6C, to provide all of our students and faculty in sixth grade access to a learning environment that is more flexible. As Jacobs and Alcock (2017) note, "The most fundamental structures in our schools are often inhibitors to progress: our schedules, our physical spaces, the grouping patterns of learners, and the configuration of the personnel" (p. 22). As we work to provide a more personalized learning experience for our students, we find that physical space is limiting our ability to do so. As most adults in our community were served well by a traditional classroom environment, parents may have some questions about why we'd make this change.

> As we work to provide a more personalized learning experience for our students, we find that physical space is limiting our ability to do so.

How does a flexible learning environment relate to personalized learning?

"Flexible learning environments imply that the school adapts the use of resources such as staff, space, and time to best support personalization" (Wall, G., 2016, p. 20). So, what does personalization mean at SAS? It's a combination of different structures, instructional strategies, and curricular approaches that allow students to have access to what they need when they need it,

Figure 8-5: *This learning suite at Singapore American School with two teachers sharing a contiguous space that used to be two separate classrooms is part of the "flexible learning environment" write-up in this chapter.*

8 CHAPTER PATHFINDERS — TAKING THE FIRST STEP

> A successful Pathfinder is the work being done by the Middle School at Singapore American School. They practice the "Build it, Live it and Own it" philosophy.

to know what their next steps are in their learning, and to pursue areas of strength and interest. We use the terms flexible learning environments, customized pathways, and competency-based progressions to frame our understanding of the elements necessary to create a personalized experience for children.

What is a flexible learning environment?

When people think of a flexible learning environment, they often think only of the physical space. While it is true that the space is flexible in nature, there is much more to a flexible learning environment than just the physical floor plan or furniture choices. Modern flexible learning environments also address other elements of the learning environment such as how students are grouped during learning and how time might be used more flexibly during the day.

Flexible Physical Space

After the renovations, the sixth grade learning communities will have a flexibility that didn't exist in the prior layout. Teachers and students can still configure the space to work in an environment similar to a traditional classroom if that is what is best for teaching and learning. However, we also know that not all learning involves 22 students in a single room at chairs and tables.

Figure 8-6: *This is a different part of the same flexible learning environment where the layout is less "classroom-like." Notice the transparency to the outdoors created when this space was renovated.*

Figure 8-7: *The Flexible Learning Environment includes spaces like this for informal work, small group instruction and independent study.*

The new learning communities feature additional flexibility, creating spaces for groups of different sizes. There are small breakout rooms throughout the space so groups of students can work collaboratively. Some examples of what might happen in the smaller breakout spaces include activities like book partnerships and literature circles, math explorations, independent work, or collaborative work on a group presentation. A teacher might also pull a group of students into a smaller breakout space to re-teach a concept or provide a lesson that extends the current concept for students who have already grasped it. There is also the ability to open the space to bring all students on a grade level team together for large group activities. Some examples of when the space would be opened up include visitors making whole group presentations to the students, or sharing learning celebrations with the community. Sixth grade math teacher Kris Munden sums it up this way: "In a traditional classroom with four walls, you're restricted by those four walls. But here we don't just have four walls, we have a bunch of walls that can open and close, so we can make the space fit what we need, rather than the space dictating what we can do."

Flexible Time

There is much more to a flexible learning environment than the physical space. The flexibility extends to the use of time. All of our middle school core teams currently have the ability to flex their schedules and often do so. What do we mean by this? Each grade level has a block of time dedicated to our core program. English/Language Arts (ELA),

> There is much more to a flexible learning environment than just the physical floor plan or furniture choices.

8 CHAPTER PATHFINDERS — TAKING THE FIRST STEP

> "Here we can make the space fit what we need, rather than the space dictating what we can do."

math, science, social studies, and PE. Teams can reorganize that scheduled block in numerous ways to allow for different uses of the time. For example, they might revise the schedule, shortening classes, to create a block of time for a guest speaker or a homebase activity. In sixth grade, they often use a schedule that shortens core blocks to create a flexible block of time after lunch. Students, with guidance from their teachers, identify what learning they want support in, and sign up for specific workshops to reinforce those skills during this block. Sometimes this might be remediation of a concept taught earlier in the day. Other times it will be an extension activity for students who have already grasped the concept from earlier in the day. At times, these blocks of time are also used to make explicit connections between the disciplines. Students may use this time to work on unit culminating projects that bring learning from multiple subjects together. These flexible blocks help students personalize their learning path, make connections across disciplines, and give them voice and choice in their learning.

Flexible Student Grouping

Traditionally, students are grouped together for a specific class at a specific time at the beginning of the year, and that grouping doesn't change. A student's classmates for ELA class, for example, remains static all year. However, this presumes that all students are the same, and need the exact same learning opportunities, at the exact same time. We know that all students are unique, and so this model has its limitations. Our teachers work closely together to plan for instruction based on student

Figure 8-8: *As part of the Flexible Learning Environment, teachers have their own space to work and plan. Notice how this is an "open office" with a "help desk" similar to an Apple "Genius Bar." The idea is that students can approach teachers and ask for help if and when they need it. This space has adjacent small group rooms visible in the picture where students can work in teams without disturbing the rest of the learning community.*

8 CHAPTER PATHFINDERS — TAKING THE FIRST STEP

Figure 8-9: *One of the Pathfinders at Singapore American School included a better integration of this Maker Space with adjacent learning areas.*

need. If a group of students needs extra time on a certain math concept, they are given that extra time during a flexible block, regardless of which math class they are scheduled into. Teachers examine students' formative work on a regular basis to identify what learning they need next. Students are then grouped and regrouped in response to that data. The research affirms this, as well: "Using data to frequently adapt student grouping strategies to student needs is a key aspect of personalization; it is yet another way that instructors can be responsive to student needs and allow students to take various paths through content" (Pane, Steiner, Baird, & Hamilton, 2015, p. 22). Regardless of whether your child will be in a renovated space or not, teams of teachers across the middle school are finding ways to focus on flexible student grouping.

Does a flexible learning environment improve learning?

When teachers are working more collaboratively, they see connections across the skills and content from their specific courses. Our survey data shows that students working in the 6A space felt that their teachers knew what was going on in other classes, and the students were more likely to make connections between subjects than those not in a flexible learning environment.

> When teachers are working more collaboratively, they see connections across the skills and content from their specific courses.

> Flexible blocks of time help students personalize their learning path, make connections across disciplines, and give them voice and choice in their learning.

Interdisciplinary planning and conversations allow teachers to develop common language for skills that transcend subject areas. For example, writing a claim, supporting it with evidence, and using reasoning occurs in almost all subject areas, though not always in the exact same format. In a flexible learning environment, teachers more easily calibrate their language, and students make overt connections between subject area content and skills. While this may not show up explicitly in a standardized test result, students build their ability to see the world as inter-connected, which we know it is. In fact, the creation of disconnected subjects for schools goes back to 1892, when the National Education Association in New York "set public school institutions onto a pathway of discipline divisions" (Jacobs and Alcock, 2017, p. 65). Since we don't experience the world in discrete subjects, it makes sense that we set up opportunities so students won't either. Additionally, using flexible grouping and time allows students to be pushed further in their areas of strength and to get additional time and support in areas of challenge. A study by the Rand Corporation indicates "that compared to their peers, students in schools using personalized learning practices are making greater progress over the course of two school years, and that students who started out behind are now catching up to perform at or above national averages" (Pane et. al, 2015, p. 34).

How does a flexible learning environment increase teacher effectiveness?

We all have partnerships in our lives that increase our effectiveness—maybe it is a co-worker who helps us see things at work we might not otherwise see, or a spouse, who shares responsibility for parenting. Working closely with someone on a common goal (increasing performance at work, or raising children to be good humans) enhances our lives. We make better decisions and perform better when we have a partner, or team to support us. The same happens with teachers. When they are working more collaboratively together, the benefits are substantial. Teachers learn from each other and get more regular feedback on their instructional practices. The level of transparency in a more flexible environment encourages teachers to work at the highest level possible. Some say that the flexible environment ensures they bring their "A game" daily. The teachers feel a sense of collective responsibility for all students' learning.

Figure 8-10: *SAS put up these "posters" describing the enhanced learning spaces represented by the Pathfinders. The initial pathfinders directly impacted only a relatively small number of students in a 4,000-student school. So there was value in publicizing the effort to the whole school community before scaling up and replicating the philosophy, pedagogy and curriculum practiced in the pathfinder spaces.*

8 CHAPTER PATHFINDERS — TAKING THE FIRST STEP

PATHFINDER RATING SCALE — EFFICACY OF TEACHING AND LEARNING

Use this Form to Evaluate the Efficacy of any Lesson or Learning Activity in the Proposed Pathfinder Space During a Specified Block of Time Before and After Pathfinder is Created

Activity	Description	Weight*	TRUE	Partially True	Not True	Weighted Score
			2	1	0	
Independent Work	Assignment has opportunities for students to work independently	4				
Small Teams	Assignment has opportunities for students to work in small teams of 2 to 5	7				
Variety of Technologies	Various technologies are present and in use by students without teacher assistance	6				
Student-Centered	The majority of the work is done by students with a mimimal amount of direct instruction	5				
Student-Directed	Students have "agency" meaning that they decide what, when, where and how to learn	8				
Teacher as Coach	Teachers mostly observe from the sidelines and provide help only when requested by students	10				
Multiple Groupings	The space is designed to accommodate student groupings of different sizes	6				
Flexible Schedule	The schedule is designed to allow students to spend time doing work without constant interruption	9				
Indoor-Outdoor Work	Space is designed so students can work outside on good days	4				
Interdisciplinary	There is an interdisciplinary component in student work	5				
Hands-on Work	Students have an opportunity to apply their theoretical knowledge with hands-on work	6				
Assessment	Assessment is geared to measure the extent to which students are using and improving essential life skills	8				
Teacher Collaboration	The spaces are designed to afford opportunities for teachers to collaborate and work together	10				

*These are suggested weights only. Each school or school district should adjust weights based on their own priorities	Excellent	85% - 100%	Actual Score	
	Very Good	70% - 90%	Maximum Possible Score	176
	Acceptable	50% - 70%	Actual Score as a Percentage of Maximum Possible Score	
	Unacceptable — Needs Work	30% - 50%	*Pathfinder Rating Scale* © Fielding Nair International	
	Poor — Needs Substantial Changes	Below 30%		

Figure 8-11: *The Pathfinder Evaluation Tool can be most helpful when it is used as a way to benchmark the overall educational effectiveness of an existing space before and after a Pathfinder is created. This tool serves as a mechanism to design great educational experiences for students regardless of what they are learning. It is a seamless blend of curriculum, pedagogy, schedule, student autonomy, teacher collaboration and assessment. It provides a quantifiable measure of what are, essentially, qualitative elements that profoundly impact teaching and learning.*

References:

Jacobs, H. H., & Alcock, M. (2017). Bold moves for schools: How we create remarkable learning environments. Alexandria, VA, USA: ASCD.

Pane, J., Steiner, E., Baird, M., & Hamilton, L. (2015). Continued Progress: Promising Evidence on Personalized Learning. doi:10.7249/rr1365

Wall, G. (2016). The Impact of Physical Design on Student Outcomes (New Zealand, Department of Education). Retrieved from https://www.education.govt.nz/assets/Documents/Primary-Secondary/Property/School-property-design/Flexible-learning-spaces/FLS-The-impact-of-physical-design-on-student-outcomes.pdf

> The level of transparency in a more flexible environment encourages teachers to work at the highest level possible.

The Pathfinder Evaluation Tool

In theory, it makes sense for a school to try out an innovative new approach at a small scale before rolling it out across the whole school. However, in practice, this still begs the big question. "How do we know it will work?" And the follow-up questions, once the Pathfinder or Pathfinders are built, are "How can we know it works?" and "How much better is this than what we had before?"

As we have stated throughout this book, learning spaces influence what we learn, how we learn it, and how well we learn. However, learning spaces, in and of themselves, are only a part of the story. The true efficacy of a learning space can only be determined when its potential as a learning resource is fully exploited by the teachers and students who occupy it. This is no different than any learning resource. A computer that sits unopened in the box or gets put on a desk without Internet access can never be as effective as one whose potential to connect the learner with the world of information and people online can be.

We developed the "Pathfinder Evaluation Tool" featured in this book (and also available as an APP for your mobile device) that is a hybrid tool that evaluates the quality and use of the learning space in the context of how ancillary elements like schedule and assessments are also being leveraged to maximize the value of the built environment.

The Pathfinder Evaluation Tool can be most helpful when it is used as a way to benchmark the overall educational effectiveness of an existing space before and after a Pathfinder is created. This tool serves as a mechanism to design great educational experiences for students regardless of what they are learning. It is a seamless blend of curriculum, pedagogy, schedule, student autonomy, teacher collaboration, and assessment. It provides a quantifiable measure of what are, essentially, qualitative elements that profoundly impact teaching and learning. In the process, this tool can provide the hard "data" schools need to justify larger scale, campus-wide renovation projects and building additions.

> The Pathfinder Evaluation Tool can be most helpful when it is used as a way to benchmark the overall educational effectiveness of an existing space before and after a Pathfinder is created.

CHAPTER 9
SCALING UP CHANGE — THE STORY OF BOULDER VALLEY SCHOOLS

This book focuses on a new and improved model of education, one that is grounded solidly in learning research that is cited throughout this book and spelled out in great detail by Dr. Richard Elmore in Part Two — Chapter 11. In doing so, it suggests new ways to structure schools that are very different than the way most schools are currently designed. It recommends supplanting the "classroom" construct model and moving, instead, to a "Learning Community" model where students are free to choose from a variety of modalities of learning like independent study, peer tutoring, team collaboration, research, and presentations and teachers are provided with a more robust palette of instructional opportunities than would have been afforded in a traditionally designed school building.

> This book suggests new ways to structure schools that are very different than the way most schools are currently designed, set up and operate.

The rationale behind the many ideas presented here are difficult to contest because they are supported by the vast majority of educators themselves. However, that doesn't mean changing the educational model from teacher-centered to student-centered and from classroom-based to community-based is easy. Even exclusive private schools that exist in highly competitive markets struggle with change. It is reasonable to expect that changes will be even more difficult when they have to be applied across multiple schools across an entire school district and that is, indeed, true. However, this chapter has been included in this book to show that while larger scale change is difficult, it is not impossible.

Over the next several years, thousands of schools across the country will need upgrading if only because of their age and physical condition. Tens of billions of dollars in capital construction expenditures will, inevitably, be made to bring schools into a state of good repair. It is our contention that this spending represents a huge opportunity to address the future of education so that new and renovated school buildings become true manifestations of a new educational model. An

> It is reasonable to expect that changes will be even more difficult when they have to be applied across multiple schools across an entire school district.

Figure 9-1: *Meadowlark School, Boulder Valley School District's first school in Erie, Colorado, serves students in PK through 8th grade. The school is a dynamic learning environment organized into five learning communities. The innovative educational spaces provided in the building's footprint promote collaboration and partnerships for all stakeholders.*
Message from Principal Brent Caldwell and Assistant Principal Sennen Knauer.
Photo © Fred J. Fuhrmeister.

> "
> The Educational Innovation portion of the Bond program in BVSD is a great example of what can be achieved when a community supports their schools by leveraging facilities improvement as a catalyst to foster Innovative instructional practices.

educational model that is more in tune with today's needs than the one that continues to be delivered in row-upon-row of similarly sized classrooms.

Boulder Valley School District (BVSD) was courageous enough to do just that. BVSD has 31,000 students housed in 56 schools located in communities near and including Boulder, Colorado in the United States. They recognized that the $576 million they had raised via a bond referendum to build and renovate their schools could be leveraged not only to provide better places for their students to learn in, but also provide teachers with the opportunity to practice a different instructional model — one that would be more collaborative and interdisciplinary. Much of the bond money was already allocated to address much-needed architectural, engineering and structural improvements at their various schools. The bond budget included funding to build three new elementary schools and one K-8 school, and do major renovations at several other schools including middle and high schools. There was also a discretionary fund of approximately $20 million dollars that was set aside to fund innovative programs at various schools. To access the funds, each school developed an Innovation Project Plan that demonstrated how their expenditure of capital funds would have direct educational benefits. These funds could only be accessed by schools that could demonstrate how their expenditure of capital funds would have direct educational benefits. Some of these are outlined in the section below.

> We wanted to understand the extent to which teachers feel their innovative learning environment has contributed to their ability to deliver on the district's high level aspirations represented by their "Innovation Guiding Principles."

In this chapter, we have invited Kiffany Lychock, Director of Educational Innovations, to present the Boulder Valley story from the perspective of the school district. We also asked BVSD to survey their teachers who are working in the new and renovated facilities. We wanted to understand the extent to which teachers feel their innovative learning environment has contributed to their ability to deliver on the district's high level aspirations represented by their "Innovation Guiding Principles." The survey data from the school district is presented here as well with the caveat that it shows where teachers are less than one year into a fairly significant shift in their practice. We are certain that this same survey, taken two or three years down the road when the new learning model becomes the norm, rather than something teachers are still adjusting to, will show an even more positive correlation between learning spaces and instructional practices.

INNOVATIVE SPACE AS A CATALYST FOR INSTRUCTIONAL CHANGE

How Innovation and Construction Dollars have Shifted the Story of Learning in BVSD

By Kiffany Lychock, BVSD Director of Educational Innovations[66]

In architecture it is said that form follows function. This is most certainly the case with Boulder Valley School District (BVSD) schools, where we are building learning environments for the future, inspired by the innovative teaching of our educators.

> School construction spending represents a huge opportunity to address the future of education so that new and renovated school buildings become true manifestations of a new educational model.

---

[66] Special thanks and acknowledgement to the following BVSD staff that contributed to or supported the writing of this article: Susan Cousins, Randy Barber, Adam Galvin, Cece Davis, Francine Eufemia, Jon Wolfer, Samantha Messier, Rob Price, David Eggen, and Stephanie Schroeder.

9 CHAPTER SCALING UP CHANGE — THE STORY OF BOULDER VALLEY SCHOOLS

Figure 9-2: *The renovation of the Centaurus building provides the opportunity to rethink how we build schools to support student success in the 21st century. Centaurus has been identified to be an exemplar of educational innovation in the school district. It will serve as a model of 21st century approaches to teaching and learning as well as an innovative learning environment that will bring to life BVSD's Strategic Plan and BVSD's Innovation Guiding Principles.*
Building For Student Success. https://bond.bvsd.org/projects/Centaurus/Pages/default.aspx

The Educational Innovation portion of the "Building for Student Success" Bond program in BVSD is a great example of what can be achieved when a community supports their schools by leveraging facilities improvement as a catalyst to foster Innovative instructional practices.

Boulder Valley taxpayers passed a $576 million dollar bond in 2014. While half of those funds were set aside to repair and maintain safe, healthy, and comfortable buildings for students, another focus of the Bond Program was to create learning environments that support innovative approaches to instruction.

> " The focus of Boulder Valley's Bond Program was to create learning environments that support innovative approaches to instruction.

Teacher and student collaboration is at the heart of the Learning Community philosophy discussed at the start of this chapter. This is a big shift from BVSD's traditionally designed schools that had hallways surrounded by individual classrooms that were all the same size. This type of environment was built for an educational experience of teacher directed, lecture style learning. Rethinking how we can innovatively design schools to maximize the quality of spaces to better serve teaching and learning needs has empowered us to support many different modes of learning. There are spaces that work well for learning from an expert (more "traditional" lecture-style teaching), collaborative spaces where students can work in small groups to learn from each other, presentation spaces, teacher collaboration rooms, spaces that allow for individuals to work and reflect quietly, and gathering spaces for the larger community. The goal is to have learning environments that can be agile and multi-functional depending on the learning needs of the students. Innovative Learning Environments remove the barriers that traditionally designed buildings create and allow students and teachers to access a broader spectrum of opportunities as referenced in Chapter 1 of this book.

> Innovative Learning Environments remove the barriers that traditionally designed buildings create and allow students and teachers to access a broader spectrum of opportunities.

Today, just a few short years since the bond was approved, Boulder Valley has built four new schools and renovated several existing buildings to facilitate a student-centered teaching and learning model that would have been nearly impossible to implement in the older buildings.

Following the decision to leverage bond funding to create state-of-the-art learning environments, BVSD selected Fielding Nair

Figure 9-3: *Emerald is a neighborhood school with a balance of diversity that mirrors the real world. During the 2016-17 school year, the school was completely rebuilt and Emerald 2.0 opened in August of 2017. The new building features an innovative learning environment, access to the outdoors and natural light, and completely updated technology. We believe building positive relationships and explicitly teaching our four magical words (Focus, Integrity, Respect, and Empathy) to every student are critical for maximum learning to take place.*
https://www.bvsd.org/elementary/emerald/Pages/emerald.aspx

International (FNI), a world-renowned design firm, as the Design Architect for all four of the new schools and two renovation projects. FNI partnered with a local architect for each of the new schools.[67]

As its first order of business, the architects and educational consultants from FNI worked closely with BVSD to define the larger school community's aspirations for the future of education and the best ways these aspirations could be realized through the building program. The leadership team engaged in a collaborative visioning process that involved representatives from key stakeholder groups such as students, teachers, parents, administrators, and district educational leaders. This process resulted in the creation of the school district's "Innovation Guiding Principles" that were then used to drive the whole process of planning, designing, constructing and operating the new and renovated schools.

BVSD Innovation Guiding Principles that Drove the Design of its New and Renovated Schools

1. **Learning is founded in inquiry:** We believe that learning is a journey inspired by authentic questions. Along the journey of inquiry, learners acquire knowledge, abilities, ways of thinking, and skills that shape them for the next journey. Inquiry can be initiated by facilitators seeking to guide the journey learners towards specific knowledge and skills, or more ideally, originate with the learner. We will foster a culture in which questions are as important as answers, and every learner is challenged/encouraged to inquire.

2. **Learning fosters a culture of curiosity and risk-taking:** We believe that in order to succeed, we must try first. In the pursuit of understanding, learners must have the opportunity, guidance, and encouragement to take appropriate risks – expanding the limits of what they know and can do, or what might be the status quo. We support risk taking, big and small, for learners of all ages in the process of learning. We actively create a culture where curiosity is valued above rote memorization and failure in the pursuit of understanding is valued above complacency in the process of attainment.

> In the pursuit of understanding, learners must have the opportunity, guidance, and encouragement to take appropriate risks.

---

[67] Local architect at Meadowlark: Cuningham Group, Emerald: RB +B, Creekside: Bennet, Wagner, Grody, Douglass: RTA, Summit MS: Cunningham Group, Centaurus HS: GKK Works.

Figure 9-4: *An oft overlooked but critically important part of all schools is a welcoming school entrance such as this one at Emerald Elementary School in Boulder Valley. This space serves as the "heart" of the school, provides a warm and comfortable place for both students and visitors, has a working fireplace and leads directly to a magnificently daylit and easily accessible curiosity center.*
Photo © Paul Brokering.

3. **Mastery of learning is demonstrated in multiple ways:** We believe there are many ways to demonstrate deep understanding and mastery of skills. Learners develop skills and demonstrate what they know in ways that others can see, understand, and build upon. Learners are challenged to present their understanding verbally, visually, digitally, and by completing projects in multiple mediums. Facilitators of learning and learners themselves will use a variety of tools and measure their skills and understandings in multiple ways.

9 CHAPTER SCALING UP CHANGE — THE STORY OF BOULDER VALLEY SCHOOLS

Figure 9-5: *Curiosity Centers such as this one at Emerald Elementary School are wonderful examples of spaces that engage students in inquiry. Curiosity Centers take the idea of the library to a whole new level by providing access not only to books but also a variety of technologies that encourage students to produce and create and not just consume information.*

4. **Learning is a social process:** We believe learning requires interaction. When learning takes place in isolation, there is no opportunity for interaction with thoughts of others. By providing opportunities for collaboration, students use the thinking of others to inspire, improve and reflect on their own learning. Learners will seek highly effective collaboration that produces deeper, meaningful learning. We aspire to foster a culture that encourages meaningful interaction, builds communities where all learners feel safe, heard, and valued.

5. **Learning is powerful when students create solutions to authentic challenges that impact their local, national, or global community:** We believe the real world is the most relevant context in which to learn. When learners apply their knowledge and skills to challenges that impact the world they live in, they are more likely to be interested in what they are learning. Learning within authentic contexts provides students with a greater sense of purpose to their learning. We design and facilitate academically rigorous learning experiences, projects, case-studies, internships, and service learning that give learners the opportunity to make an impact on their immediate and broader communities.

6. **Learning is personalized and learner led:** We recognize the importance of learners developing skills and capacities to exercise high levels of self-management, ownership, and accountability over their own learning. We provide learning experiences which emphasize student autonomy, choice, self-assessment, multiple iterations, active exploration, and a variety of learning modalities. Teaching methods emphasize foundation building, structured guidance, facilitation, peer-to-peer teaching and

> " Innovation Guiding Principles are aspirational statements, that serve as the District's guideposts for both the new schools and renovated projects.

Figure 9-6: *Curiosity Centers do have books, and they also have access to a variety of digital tools and resources to help them investigate and research. One of our principals refers to it as "a library on steroids" – Kiffany Lychock.*

The move to Curiosity Centers was done in Boulder Valley in a way that continues to celebrate all the reasons why libraries worked in the past. They are places where students have agency, a quiet place to relax and, most of all, enjoy the companionship of a great book in a comfortable environment.
Curiosity Center at Meadowlark School.

review, connections with community, and other strategies designed to make learning meaningful, relevant, engaging and effective.

The Innovation Guiding Principles are aspirational statements that serve as the District's guideposts for both the new schools and renovated projects. The newly designed schools are referred to as "Blueprint Schools" since they have become the District's blueprint for Innovative Learning Spaces and Innovative Instruction. The name "Blueprint Schools" was derived from the book, Blueprint for Tomorrow, which provides a strong rationale for linking innovative educational spaces with innovative teaching

9 CHAPTER SCALING UP CHANGE — THE STORY OF BOULDER VALLEY SCHOOLS

Figure 9-7, 9-8: *Hallways were widened at Summit Middle School in Boulder Valley so that they could serve as breakout areas for the adjacent learning studios. See how this approach makes the previously unusable hallway a fully functional space that can be used throughout the school day.*

9 CHAPTER SCALING UP CHANGE — THE STORY OF BOULDER VALLEY SCHOOLS

and learning practices.[68]

Special acknowledgement of our building level leadership at our "Blueprint Schools" is absolutely well deserved as the principals and assistant principals have led the day to day charge during implementation.[69]

The following are examples of how these Innovation Guiding Principles were used in designing both our Blueprint schools, and in our renovation projects:

> The newly designed schools are referred to as "Blueprint Schools" since they have become the District's blueprint for Innovative Learning Spaces and Innovative Instruction.

In our Blueprint Schools

The Curiosity Centers in each of our new schools are wonderful examples of spaces that engage students in inquiry. With the advent of the Information Age and the dramatic increase in accessibility to information via the Internet, school libraries have had to redefine how they support student learning.

Our new Curiosity Centers do have books, and they also have access to a variety of digital tools and resources to help the investigate and research. One of our principals refers to it as "a library on steroids."

In addition to resources for research, our Curiosity Centers also include access to MakerSpace areas where kids inquire through design and creation. These MakerSpaces often include 3D printers, robotics, and access to green screens and digital recording equipment.

Creekside Elementary has adopted the Guiding Principle about fostering curiosity as part of their school motto, "Cultivating Curiosity."

The school kicked off their inaugural year

by challenging students and teachers to use the MakerSpace equipment to explore student curiosities. This year, the

---

[68] Blueprint for Tomorrow: Redesigning Schools for Student-Centered Learning by Prakash Nair. Harvard Education Press. 2014

[69] Thank you to Samara Williams, Francine Eufemia, Jon Wolfer, Brent Caldwell, Sennen Knauer, Adam Galvin, Cece Davis, and Dan Ryan for their leadership and passion.

Figure 9-9: *Cafeterias such as this one at Meadowlark School contain all the comforts of a good coffee shop with the added advantage of some amazing mountain views.*
Photo © Fred J. Fuhrmeister.

staff is focused more on creating a "Maker Culture" and are working to expand the use of the MakerSpace tools into the Learning Communities and other commons areas of the school to enhance instruction across all academic areas.

In addition to fostering inquiry, our Curiosity Centers are an obvious support for this IGP as well. Having access to print and digital information, as well as digital tools, students are able to explore their curiosities through reading and research.

In terms of risk-taking, our new buildings that are founded in a learning community model have challenged our district and building leaders, and especially our teachers, to take significant risks in rethinking their instructional practices. It has been a significant second order change, which has presented us with numerous opportunities for successes and also had its fair share of failures. These failures, however, have allowed us to regroup, rethink and recharge, with the goal of stretching our thinking to provide more innovative learning opportunities for our students.

In our Renovation Projects:

Whittier International Elementary, a longstanding International Baccalaureate Primary Years Program (IB PYP), has always been focused on transdisciplinary units that allow students to take ownership of their learning and take action in their world.

Whittier used their innovation funds to invest in mobile, flexible furniture and seating options in order to have a wider variety of spaces to match instructor and learner needs. The teachers wanted the ability to quickly and fluidly shift from a learning environment that is set up for individual work time, to spaces that support collaborative grouping for a variety of group sizes.

The new furniture has created an opportunity for the learning environment to better match the aims of the transdisciplinary units of study so students now have agency and choice in what they learn as well as where, or in what environment, they learn. The learning environment resulting from this project has enhanced the IB PYP and the effects are visible daily in the classrooms at Whittier. As the principal noted once the furniture was in place, "The bathrooms used to be full of the buzz of students taking breaks from learning. Since construction, the bathrooms are quiet and the classrooms are buzzing as students' needs for movement and flexibility while learning is being met by the new furniture."

Aspen Creek K-8 created new learning dens in their elementary area, redesigned their library, created a distance learning lab, and repurposed a computer lab into a MakerSpace they call their "Think Tank," to give students access to spaces where they can create, invent, and try out new ideas.

The school sought to provide places and opportunities for student led experimentation

> The school sought to provide places and opportunities for student led experimentation zones where kids could invent, make, and deconstruct to fuel their learning.

Figure 9-10: *New and renovated school projects provide an interesting opportunity to "look behind the walls and under the floors" so that students can see how the building is actually engineered. Elements of electrical, mechanical and plumbing systems can be exposed and become the subject of both formal and informal education in the school.*
Meadowlark School.
Photo © Fred J. Fuhrmeister.

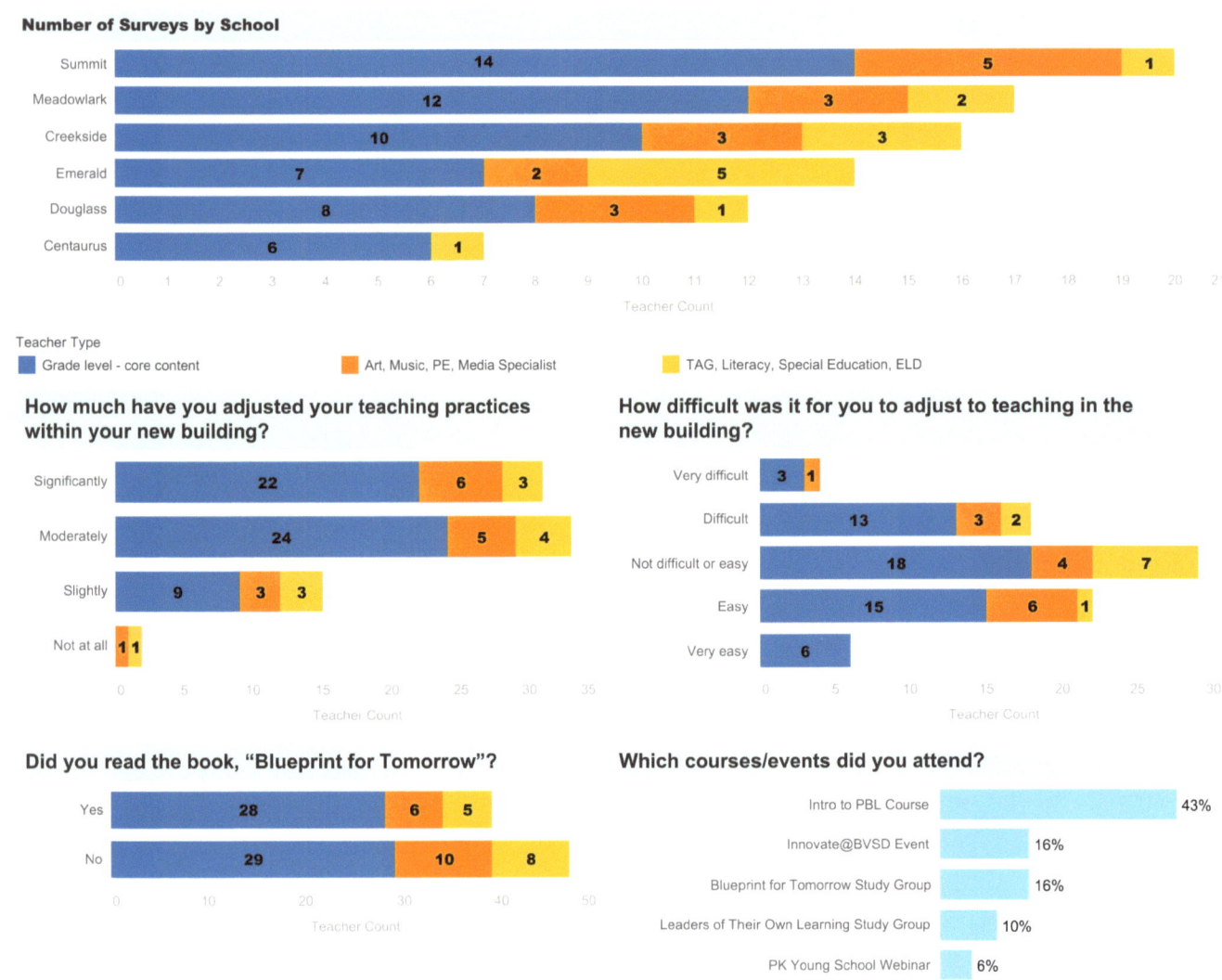

Figure 9-11: Boulder Valley School District. Results of teacher surveys to gauge the effectiveness of six new and renovated schools. Part One.

zones where kids could invent, make, and deconstruct to fuel their learning. Including spaces to display ongoing student work to inspire ideas for others was another project goal. Flexible zones where the process of curiosity and design were built to support students as they engaged in exploration and creation during their learning.

These are but a few of the dozens of innovative practices inspired by BVSD's Guiding Principles that the various new and renovated schools in Boulder Valley have adopted.[70]

At the time of this writing, the new and renovated schools at BVSD had just begun their second school year in their new buildings and, already, there is significant evidence that innovative, student-centered educational practices will flourish when students and teachers are afforded the opportunity to work in Innovative Learning Environments.

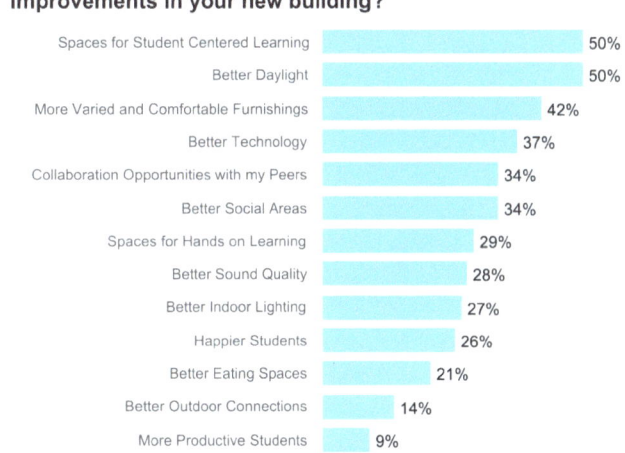
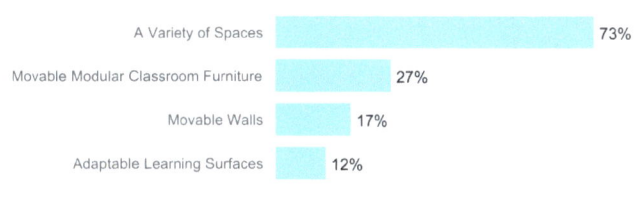
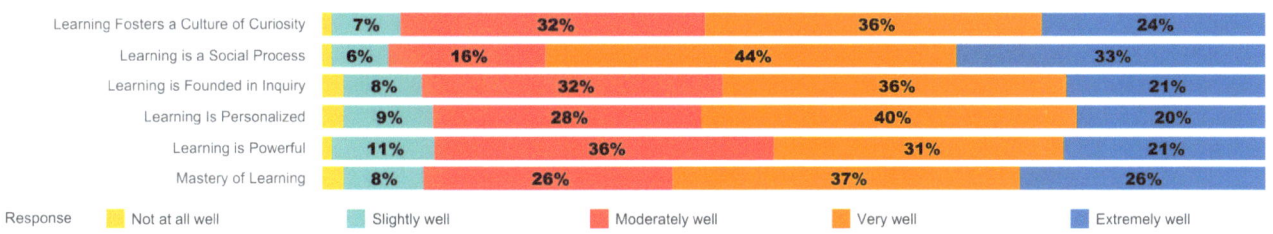

Figure 9-12: *Boulder Valley School District. Results of teacher surveys to gauge the effectiveness of six new and renovated schools. Part Two.*

---

[70] For more detail, please see this book's website at LearningByDesign.co

BVSD Teacher Survey Results

In the lead-up to writing this chapter for the book, we asked BVSD to survey their teachers to gauge the effectiveness of their new and renovated school buildings from the perspective of teaching and learning. The results from the survey are in and they are illustrated by the graphs and charts included here. The following summarizes the results of the teacher survey:

1. A total of 86 teachers at six new and renovated schools participated in the survey.

2. 53% of all teachers and 100% of core subject teachers say they have adjusted their teaching significantly or moderately as a result of their move into the new learning spaces.

3. 74% of all teachers said that they did not find it difficult to transition to the new space that permitted them many new opportunities to teach and learn.[71]

4. Teachers identified a number of learning-related building improvements that they experienced. At the top of their list were: Spaces for Student Centered Learning, Improved Daylighting and More Varied and Comfortable Furnishings

5. Teachers felt that the elements that most positively impact student learning are: A Variety of Spaces and Movable, Modular Furniture

6. Between 97% to 99% of teachers felt that the new and renovated school buildings facilitated the implementation of the six Innovation Guiding Principles.

The results show that BVSD has had success in leveraging their capital construction program to advance their educational vision. BVSD executed this program in a thoughtful, methodical and inclusive way so that their entire school community could work hand-in-hand with the architects and professional development teams before, during and after construction. There is evidence that, as teachers get more familiar and comfortable in their new spaces, it will continue to positively influence their teaching practice and student learning. Student achievement will, inevitably, improve as well — not just against traditional measures like standardized test scores but, more importantly, with regard to them gaining and building on valuable skills like complex problem solving, critical thinking and creativity.[72]

---

[71] The ease with which teachers adjusted to the new spaces is explained by the fact that all of them were provided with access to a number of Professional Development opportunities via courses and study events that the vast majority of them participated in.
[72] For more information on BVSD's Innovation work, please visit bvsdinnovation.org

CHAPTER 10
NEW DIRECTIONS FOR A NEW WORLD

Taken together, the implementation of the ideas presented in this book can lead to a brave and dramatic turnaround of entire schools, school systems and, indeed, education itself. That, unfortunately, is not how change happens. Real and lasting change often begins with small-scale innovations that can operate within the bounds of education as we know it. This is illustrated in our discussion about Pathfinders in Chapter Eight. In this Chapter, we will elaborate further about some innovative ideas that are leading the way. This discussion is not intended to be a comprehensive treatise on all the great innovations that

Figure 10-1: *Matthew Haas, now Superintendent of ACPS (left) and Isaac Williams (center) discuss the study's preliminary findings, and the details of the scenarios being considered during a community town hall and "pin up" of the scenarios.*

10 CHAPTER NEW DIRECTIONS FOR A NEW WORLD

> "Albemarle County Public Schools in the United States took a hard look at their plans to build a new high school and decided that there was a better way."

are happening in schools around the world and is provided here merely as a primer for further study and research.

In the following essay by Isaac Williams we see how one school district in the United States took a hard look at their plans to build a new High School and decided that there was a better way to address their projected enrollment increase.

A VISION FOR THE FUTURE OF HIGH SCHOOL

A Network Of Resources

By Isaac Williams, Partner, Fielding Nair International

Albemarle County Public Schools (ACPS), in Virginia, USA, is the first learning community we have designed at a district-wide scale. ACPS is an interesting case study of how by thinking differently about what learning should look like for older students, a different vision can emerge for what high school can and should look like.

Albemarle County is in many ways a microcosm of the United States. At 726 square miles, it is large geographically, with a few larger towns and cities like Charlottesville, and many rural areas in between. It is economically and racially diverse and seeks to address many similar challenges and inequities there that are present across the country. ACPS is, therefore, an interesting case study about systemic change that will be applicable in many similarly sized towns and cities in America.

ACPS commissioned a planning study to address enrollment growth in the suburbs surrounding Charlottesville. Demographic data suggested that over the next 10 years an influx of high school students from the growing suburbs in the north and west of Charlottesville would begin to

Figure 10-2: *A community member studies the findings up close.*

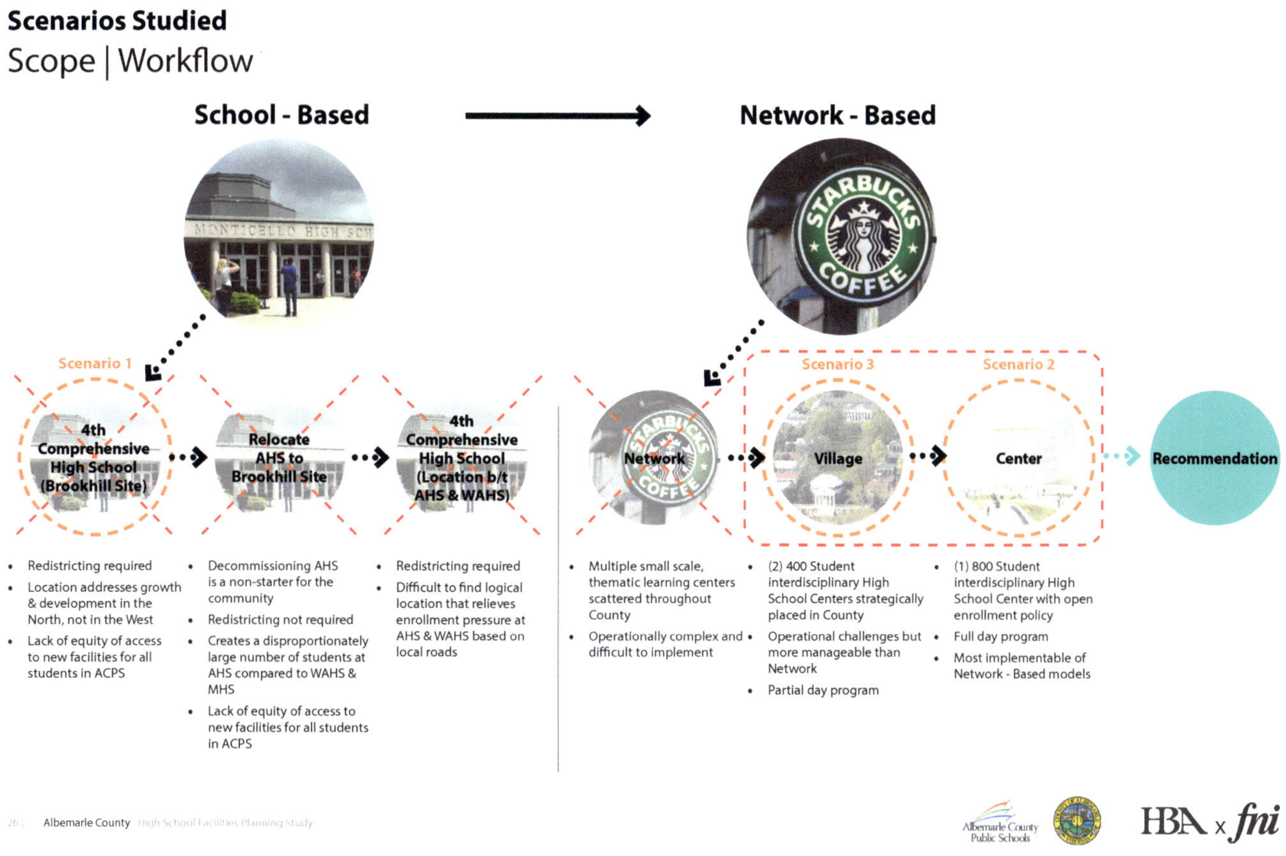

10 CHAPTER NEW DIRECTIONS FOR A NEW WORLD

Figure 10-3: *A range of scenarios were studied from a fourth Comprehensive High School, to a range of small-scale thematic learning centers placed around the county.*

overcrowd at least two of its four main high schools. There was talk of creating a fifth high school to the northwest of Charlottesville in an affluent suburb, and land there had already been proffered to the county. ACPS, led by Superintendent Pam Moran, nationally recognized as a leader in creative thinking about the role space can play in the learning process, wisely expanded the study to include the entire portfolio of high schools, so that district-wide solutions could be considered.

We began our work with ACPS by imagining a prototypical schedule for an ACPS student in the future, based on a video ACPS had published that illustrated a vision for the Day in the Life of high school students in 2022[73]. The video brilliantly captured a collection of experiences from advanced project work in the high school to internships and apprenticeships in the community, all in a more flexible, expanded schedule from 8 am well into the night.

> **"**
> The High School Centers would be gateways to community connections and partnerships with local industry.

---

[73] High School 2022 – A Day in the Life. Albemarle County Public Schools. https://www.youtube.com/watch?v=sst80ikBc4w&feature=youtu.be

135

10 CHAPTER NEW DIRECTIONS FOR A NEW WORLD

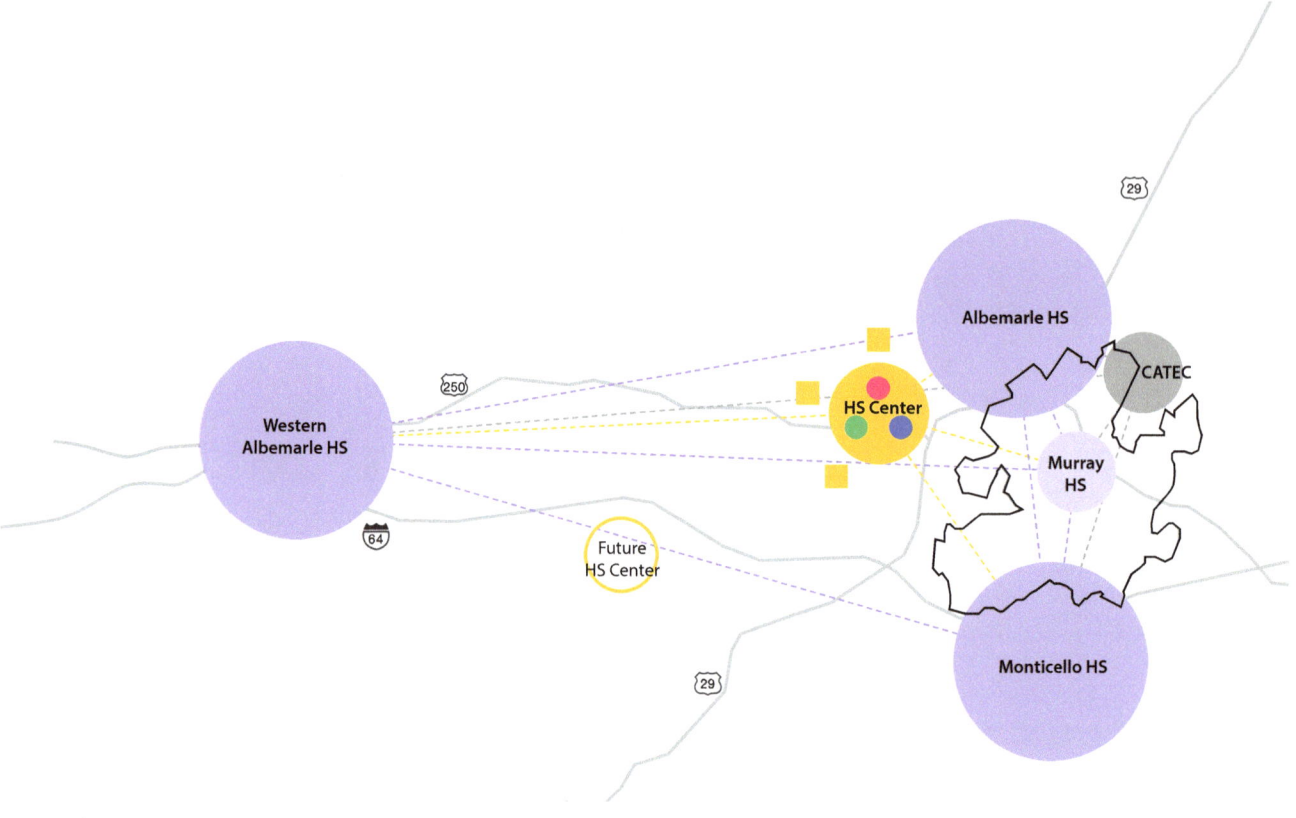

Figure 10-4: *The recommended and adopted solution, adds to two high school centers with advanced professional programs to a network of resources and programs in the community and at the existing comprehensive high schools.*

Students in the video were pursuing their passions and connecting with resources in and out of the school building that could support their work. **No longer was school a place; instead, under this scenario, it became a network of experiences and resources throughout the community.**

A Network of Resources

We then began to rethink not only the notion of high school, but the whole school system, imagining ACPS no longer as just a system of schools, but as *a network of resources*. The mission of any school district is not just to operate schools, but to educate children to become healthy, wise, and productive adults and citizens. It was clear that the traditional American comprehensive high school in a system of separate schools simply could not support the passions and interests of all students as illustrated in the High 2022 video, in much the same way that a library in 2019 cannot hold all of the books in the world. Yet, in the same way that the library can be a gateway to all the knowledge anyone could ever want, why should a student's quest for knowledge be bound by the four walls of a school building? Therefore, it no longer made sense to add a new comprehensive high school to the district with the same limitations as the other four high schools that would serve the needs of only the students fortunate enough to live near it. A new approach to school was needed.

10 CHAPTER NEW DIRECTIONS FOR A NEW WORLD

The questions then became:

- How might we connect students more directly to resources in the community that will inspire and support their growing interests?
- How might we overcome the barriers of geography and time to create equitable access for all students to the resources that will inspire and support their interests and passions?
- What might be the ideal mix between learning experiences in the high school buildings, and learning experiences in the community and how might that affect the way we think about the role of the high school building, and its capacity to deliver learning as part of a larger network of resources?

The High School Center — A Third Place

The answer to these questions came in the form of a High School Center, a sort of "third place" between community opportunities like internships and the high school buildings that offer the curricular foundation needed to develop interests, explore passions, and, ultimately, pursue advanced work. The High School Centers would offer a range of advanced specialized programs from

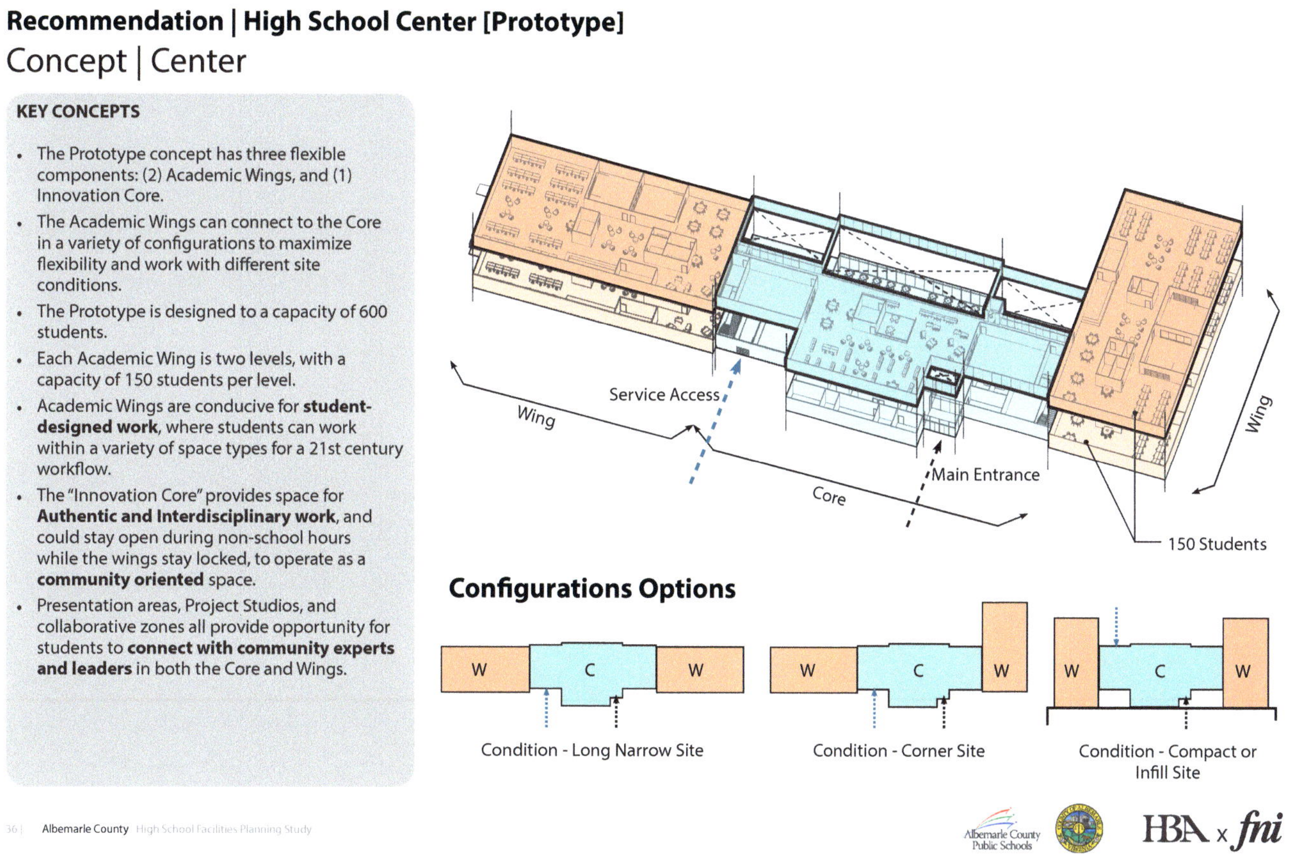

Recommendation | High School Center [Prototype]
Concept | Center

KEY CONCEPTS

- The Prototype concept has three flexible components: (2) Academic Wings, and (1) Innovation Core.
- The Academic Wings can connect to the Core in a variety of configurations to maximize flexibility and work with different site conditions.
- The Prototype is designed to a capacity of 600 students.
- Each Academic Wing is two levels, with a capacity of 150 students per level.
- Academic Wings are conducive for **student-designed work**, where students can work within a variety of space types for a 21st century workflow.
- The "Innovation Core" provides space for **Authentic and Interdisciplinary work**, and could stay open during non-school hours while the wings stay locked, to operate as a **community oriented** space.
- Presentation areas, Project Studios, and collaborative zones all provide opportunity for students to **connect with community experts and leaders** in both the Core and Wings.

Configurations Options

- Condition - Long Narrow Site
- Condition - Corner Site
- Condition - Compact or Infill Site

Figure 10-5: *Prototype for Albemarle County High School Centers, a third place between opportunities for students in the community like internships, and the home base of the comprehensive high schools.*

> We began to imagine ACPS no longer as just a system of schools, but as a network of resources.

Media and Entertainment in downtown Charlottesville, to Environmental Science and Sustainable Systems in more rural Western Albemarle. Students from all over the district would have access to the centers based on their interests. The Centers would be gateways to community connections and partnerships with local industry by providing a place where students could engage with community and business at the center rather than requiring students to traverse great distances to find opportunities. The High School Centers were strategically placed in the district based on existing hubs of business and industry, and to ensure access for students living in even the most remote areas.

With the High School Center, the existing high school was reimagined as the "home base" and foundation for 9th and 10th graders who will be exposed to a wide range of interests and opportunities through the curriculum and develop the essential skills of critical thinking, collaboration, ceativity, and communication, among others needed to pursue their passions and be successful in the long term. Building on ACPS' vision for Customized Pathways, 11th and 12th Graders would have the opportunity to branch out from the existing high schools to the High School Centers, and the community, with increasing freedom to arrange their schedule as needed to support their work. For example, a student interested in business could develop ideas for their own business at the high school center with local mentors in the morning, take a community college course in business in the evenings online, and still be in the high school band at their home high school.

ACPS' network of resources leverages the incredible learning opportunities that exist in the community now and augments them with specialized resources in the form of High School Centers to inspire and support student interests and opportunities to pursue those interests in the real world through partnerships. The vision of High School 2022, a district where every student is inspired, engaged, and has the opportunity to develop and pursue their passions, has led to a wholly different vision for high school, and how a school district operates[74].

YOUNG ENTREPRENEURS' STUDIO

Thinking Creatively and Ambitiously

In the previous section we see how the future of high schools could be very different than what we see today. That does not mean that school as a "place" cannot exist. In fact, we have written this whole book showing examples of how the place called school can become exciting and relevant again. This section provides an idea for a "Young Entrepreneurs' Studio" that be developed in a space occupied by two classrooms.

The questions that can be raised are why? Why do we need to teach entrepreneurship and why have a "studio" for it? This section will answer both questions.

"While society innovates, our K-12 schools have remained stagnant. As a result, they are not graduating the doers, makers and cutting-edge thinkers the world needs. Most institutions do not teach what should be the centerpiece of a contemporary education: entrepreneurship, the capacity

> Most institutions do not teach what should be the centerpiece of a contemporary education: entrepreneurship.

---

[74] As of this writing, the first High School Center and the modernization of the existing high schools were in design

to not only start companies but also to think creatively and ambitiously."[75]

"Entrepreneurship education benefits students from all socioeconomic backgrounds because it teaches kids to think outside the box and nurtures unconventional talents and skills. Furthermore, it creates opportunity, ensures social justice, instills confidence and stimulates the economy."[76]

Given the strong rationale for entrepreneurship education in schools, we decided to try our hand at designing a "studio" that would be dedicated to this important subject. We realized that students are truly engaged in tasks whose relevance is readily apparent. So why not have students directly engaged in developing and running their own "business"? In our drawing example we have shown a "store" that would sell the products of the business and a back office where all the work needed to run the business would happen.

Just like in any real business, this one would have a chief executive and a "staff" working on marketing, sales and finance.

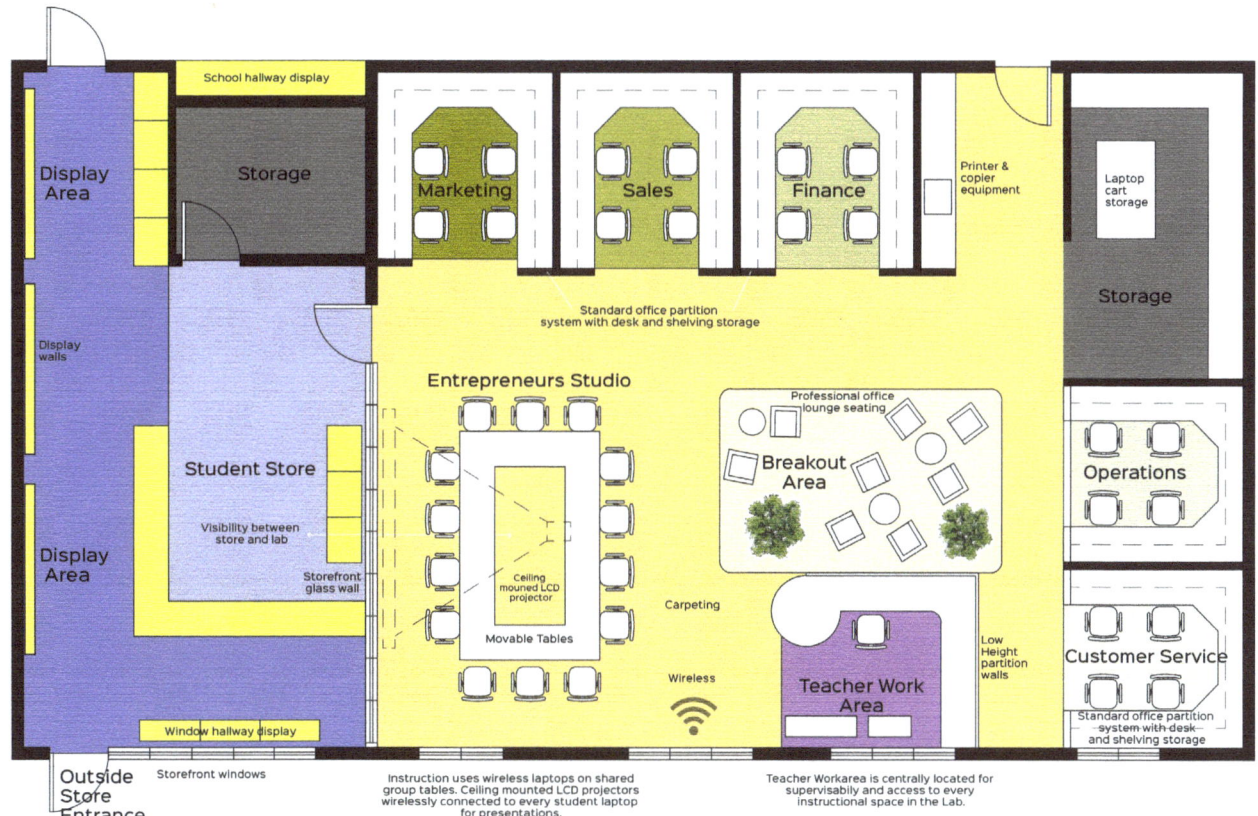

Figure 10-6: *Sketch showing a suggested layout for a Young Entrepreneurs' Studio. This studio can be constructed over the summer by combining two traditional classroom spaces.*

---

[75] Why Schools Should Teach Entrepreneurship, Entrepreneur. https://www.entrepreneur.com/article/245038
[76] Ibid

> Entrepreneurship education benefits students from all socioeconomic backgrounds because it teaches kids to think outside the box and nurtures unconventional talents and skills.

Customer service would be a priority as well. Initial "customers" may just be the school's extended community of parents and well-wishers but, if the business is successful, there is no reason why products, goods and services cannot be sold to the larger community.

This Studio would be suitable for both middle and high school students. The "curriculum" would entail all the elements that are needed to run a successful business and this can be correlated to what needs to be learned during middle school and high school. A surprising amount of content, skills and competencies that are part of the education "standards" will be automatically covered by the work needed to run a successful business. Naturally, this "course" need not be full-time, meaning that students would only work in the business on a part-time basis and they can participate in supplemental coursework as needed to fulfil their state-mandated curricular needs.

Obviously, good "teachers" for a course like this would be successful entrepreneurs from the community who may work part-time in an advisory capacity and help the students with developing and implementing their business plan. However, the role of the teacher is not to take charge of the operation but to let it run its natural course. In the real world, a vast majority of start-up businesses fail and so even if the school-based business fails, there are important lessons that students can learn.

With regard to the design and layout suggested by our sketch, this can be easily modified based on the needs of different businesses. Some are service oriented that require more of an "office" feel (which this sketch is designed to support). The student business can be production oriented, in which case the back office will become a production studio. It is largely an open space that can dynamically change with small mobile partitions and suitable furnishings as needed by the "business" the young entrepreneurs choose to plan, start and operate.

YOUNG CHEFS STUDIO

"Let food be thy medicine and medicine be thy food."

— Hippocrates

In Chapter Six, we discussed the importance of children acquiring cooking and baking skills as an important creative outlet. We also provided a strong rationale for developing these skills. Here, we are taking the idea of cooking and baking into the realm of space design. We propose a kitchen and cafe combination space that we have called the Young Chefs studio. As with the Entrepreneurs' Studio discussed above, real and meaningful learning is the byproduct of real, meaningful and rewarding work. "**Let's Get Cooking** (a network of over 5,000 school-based family cooking clubs) reports that nearly 60% of people taking part say they eat a healthier diet after being taught how to cook balanced meals. Over 9 out of 10 (92%) LGC club participants also report

> Real and meaningful learning is the byproduct of real, meaningful and rewarding work.

10 CHAPTER NEW DIRECTIONS FOR A NEW WORLD

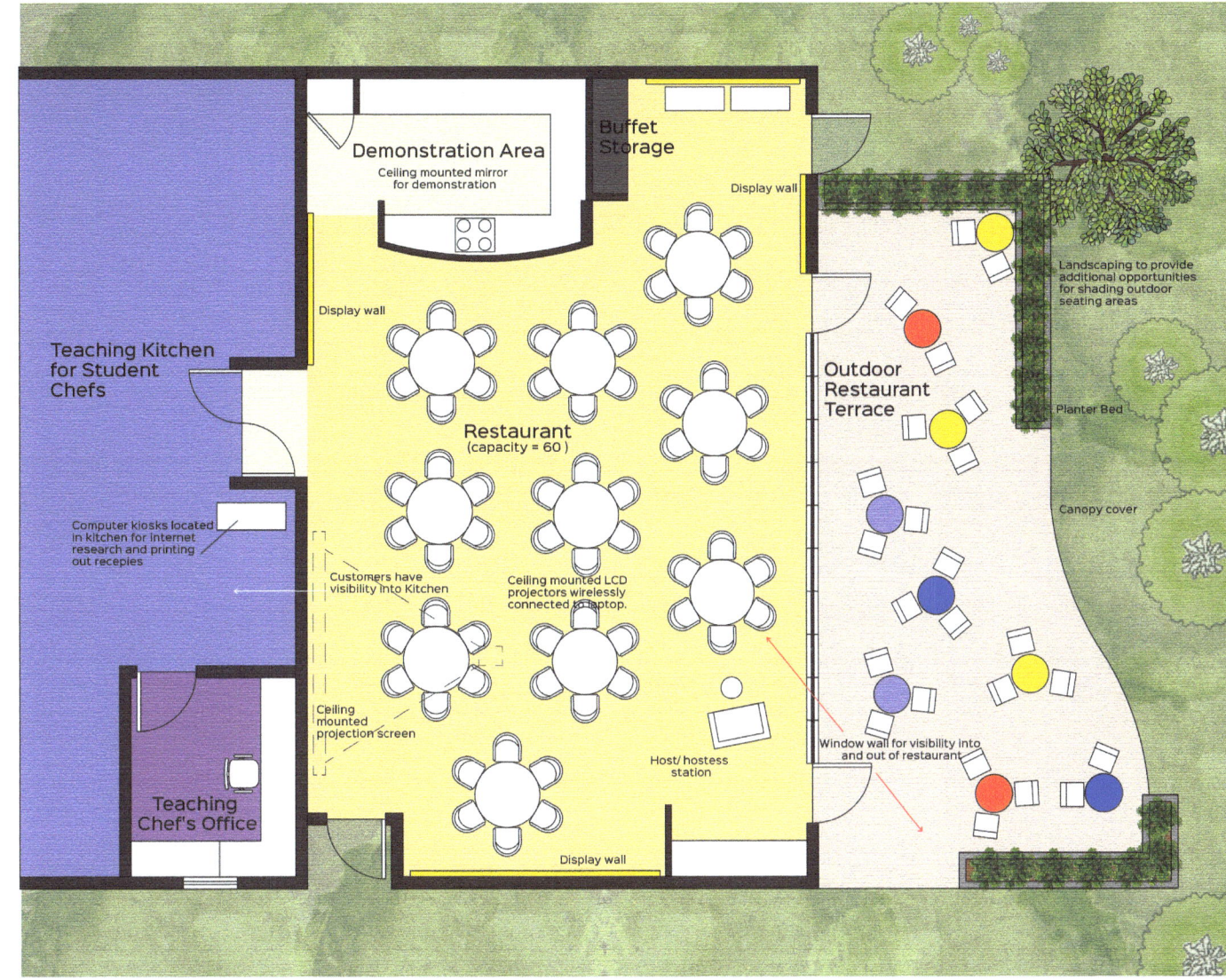

Figure 10-7: *Sketch showing a suggested layout for a Young Chefs Studio. This kind of space can be carved out of an existing school cafeteria that is adjacent to a commercial kitchen. Some modifications may be needed to the kitchen to optimize it to function as a teaching kitchen for young chefs. The outdoor eating terrace is a good feature to have but the Studio can function without it if necessary.*

regularly using their new cooking skills at home."[77]

The Young Chefs Studio can either be designed from the ground up or it can be developed with some modifications of an existing school kitchen and cafeteria. The floor plan that we have suggested here is just one approach and not intended to be read as a literal design. For example, not all schools will have the opportunity to provide an outdoor eating space adjacent to the cafe. The basic purpose is what is important. Students "learn" how to cook by working alongside a professional chef in an industrial kitchen. They are introduced to the many steps in the food preparation process and also the ancillary operations

---
[77] Why Cooking in Schools. School Food Matters. https://www.schoolfoodmatters.org/why-school-food-matters/why-cooking-schools

10 CHAPTER NEW DIRECTIONS FOR A NEW WORLD

Figure 10-8: One section of the outdoor natural learning area at the International School of Dusseldorf.

of the kitchen such as food delivery and storage, health and sanitation. The learning is not just by observation but by doing. As students advance in their culinary education, they will have opportunities to plan whole meals for large groups of people and participate in determining quantities, acquiring the proper fresh ingredients from the school farm or from the local food market, create menus and actually prepare and serve the food to real "customers." Patrons of the Young Chefs Studio can be students during the school day and community members during evenings and weekends when the school cafe can be setup to operate like a professionally run restaurant. This raises the bar on the quality that will be expected of students and, in our experience, whenever students are given this kind of responsibility and opportunity to shine, they step up and deliver.

THE SCHOOL FARM & OUTDOOR LEARNING

Beyond the Walls

In Chapter Three we touched upon the importance of gardening and taking care of animals. All schools can benefit from having programs that take the curriculum outdoors. While the benefits of outdoor learning are hard to dispute, most schools are still stuck in the mindset that

> See outdoor learning not as an add-on, but as an essential and integral part of the school's ethos and curriculum.

10 CHAPTER NEW DIRECTIONS FOR A NEW WORLD

> Most schools are stuck in the mindset that the outdoors are for relaxation and that "real" learning happens in the classroom.

the outdoors is a place to relax and connect with nature but that all the "real" learning happens inside, within the classroom. In this section, we want to highlight the value of outdoor learning not as an add-on, but as an essential and integral part of the school's ethos and curriculum. In all those cases where schools fully embrace and implement an outdoor learning component as an integral part of a student's school day, we have found students to be noticeably more engaged in their work than when they are indoors.

Here are some schools that have put in place robust outdoor learning programs where the benefits to children are readily apparent.

International School of Dusseldorf: Children at ISD use the outdoors in all kinds of weather. While they are outside they participate in a wide range of building, art and gardening activities and have the opportunity to breathe fresh air, interact with animals, socialize and play. At an event to discuss outdoor learning hosted by the school, ISD noted, "Our outdoor learning program has been developing over the last ten years. Today, our elementary school has outdoor provision from reception to grade 5. We are the only international school in Europe to have outdoor learning developed to such an extent."

Learning Gate Community School, Lutz, Florida: *Nature is our best teacher*, proclaims this school's motto. "The Learning Gate Hanna Campus is a 27-acre former orange grove that has gradually transitioned into a dense, oak forest. The campus also contains a pond, swamp and lake that are utilized for a variety of lessons and projects throughout the academic year. All students (K-5th grades) assist with the land management and monitoring of the flora/fauna that live here during their classes. Projects include invasive plant contests, tracking the reptiles/mammals species, and assisting with a migratory bird research project."[78]

Figure 10-9: "*Nature is our Best Teacher.*" Students working in the garden, which is a part of a large forested area at Learning Gate Community School, Lutz, Florida.

"The Learning Gate model focuses not only on learning about the environment but also encourages the

---
[78] https://www.learninggate.org/environment/conservation/

10 CHAPTER NEW DIRECTIONS FOR A NEW WORLD

Figure 10-10: *The Bowers School Farm is an environmentally friendly project that includes many sustainable features. The new 12,000 square foot facility uses geothermal heating, high performance insulation, septic fields, a bio-retention pond, and a fully operational greenhouse.*
Photo © by Christopher Lark.

school's surroundings and community as a framework within which students can construct their own learning. Guided by teachers and administrators using proven educational practices, they employ the environment as their comprehensive focus for learning in all areas: thinking and problem-solving skills, basic life skills, and understanding of the personal relationship to one's community and natural surroundings."[79]

Ballarat Grammar School's Mount Rowan Farm: Ballarat Grammar School in Victoria, Australia takes the concept of outdoor learning to a whole new level. They have established the dedicated Mount Rowan Farm Campus which is a 10-minute drive from their main campus. "The innovative farm campus houses the school's agriculture and horticulture studies, as well as its unique 12-month Year 4 program. The Year 4 program, based at Mt Rowan, is an innovative model with a focus on place-based learning, designed to empower students to become principled, active members of their community."[80]

Charles L. Bowers Farm, Bloomfield Hills Schools:
As with Ballarat Grammar above, The Bowers Farm in Bloomfield Hills, Michigan, is an off-site active farm that provides a rich array of resources that are not found on a typical school campus. In the words of the School District, "Charles L. Bowers School Farm was purchased in the mid-1960's by Bloomfield Hills Schools to be used as a land laboratory. We are housed on 90 acres within Bloomfield Hills.

>
> The Bowers School Farm uses geothermal heating, high performance insulation, septic fields, a bioretention pond, and a fully operational greenhouse.

---

[79] https://www.learninggate.org/environment/environmental-education/
[80] Ballarat Grammar's Mt Rowan Farm Campus gives a taste of the real world. Weekly Times
https://www.weeklytimesnow.com.au/country-living/education/secondary/ballarat-grammars-mt-rowan-farm-campus-gives-a-taste-of-the-real-world/news-story/f443d0e27d2b44d9e02f06faf8c73e7e

10 CHAPTER NEW DIRECTIONS FOR A NEW WORLD

Figure 10-11: *This picture shows Prof. Richard Elmore in a workshop at the GOGYA professional development center for AMIT, a 100-school network in Israel. Since its development a few years ago, several thousand teachers have experienced learning at this dynamically flexible center. Teachers at GOGYA learn in the same multi-faceted way in which we would expect their students to learn. Design by Fielding Nair International and Alefbet Planners.*

Animals such as sheep, horses, llama and a donkey graze the pastures. We also house poultry of all types, rabbits and goats. Every animal has a purpose here at the farm and farm equipment is used daily to maintain the property as an educational agriculture production enterprise."

"The Bowers School Farm is an environmentally friendly project that includes many sustainable features. The new 12,000 square foot facility uses geothermal heating, high performance insulation, septic fields, a bio-retention pond, and a fully operational greenhouse. Recycled wood, bamboo, low-emitting glues, adhesives and carpets as well as lighting devices that begin to dim down fixtures as exterior lighting filters into the building are other 'green' initiatives in use at the school."[81]

> Animals such as sheep, horses, llama and a donkey graze the pastures. We also house poultry of all types, rabbits and goats. Every animal has a purpose here at the farm and farm equipment is used daily to maintain the property as an educational agriculture production enterprise."

---
[81] https://www.bartonmalow.com/projects/bowers-farm

10 CHAPTER NEW DIRECTIONS FOR A NEW WORLD

PROFESSIONAL DEVELOPMENT CENTERS

Learn the Way You Intend to Teach

"The Missing Link in School Reform" is a 2011 Stanford research publication authored by Carrie R. Leana.[82] This paper provides evidence that, contrary to popular belief, reform efforts focused on improving the capabilities of individual teachers are less effective than those which engage teachers collectively. In other words, according to Ms. Leanna, "Trust and meaningful communication among teachers are the bases of true reform efforts."

If the results of this landmark study were to be directly applied to the design of school facilities, the first thing one might change is the traditional classroom which traps individual teachers in a box with little opportunity to interact with their peers. Instead of individual teachers "owning" individual classrooms, a group of teachers might own a learning community. In this community, teachers would have frequent opportunities to consult with their peers and also develop multi-age and interdisciplinary learning opportunities for students.

If this is true, then why aren't all schools rushing to develop Learning Communities in place of classrooms and why aren't teachers clarmoring to be released from the prison represented by a closed-in classroom? This is a chicken and egg problem.

Figure 10-12: *The Maker Lab at GOGYA gives teachers the same hands-on learning experiences as students would have in modern schools that are outfitted with the latest equipment and technology for creative, hands-on learning.*

---

[82] The Missing Link in School Reform by Carrie R. Leanna, Stanford Social Innovation Review
https://ssir.org/articles/entry/the_missing_link_in_school_reform

Schools have curriculums and teachers have mastered pedagogies that work best within the confines of grade-based classrooms. The reason that curriculum and pedagogy remain fixed in the past is because the traditional stand-and-deliver model of education is what the physical spaces are optimized for and any major departure from this model is, literally, impossible to do within the confines of classrooms. That means curriculums and pedagogies won't and can't change because of the physical limitations of space and school buildings remain firmly locked into the past because this kind of space best serves the prevalent education model.

> Instead of individual teachers "owning" individual classrooms, a group of teachers might own a learning community. In this community, teachers would have frequent opportunities to consult with their peers and also develop multi-age and interdisciplinary learning opportunities for students.

Compounding all this is Teacher Professional Development which, in order for it to be meaningful, trains teachers how to get the best value from their classrooms and not how to operate in a learning community. What is the use of training teachers to work in learning communities if they are unable to apply these ideas when they get back to their classroom-based schools? This is only a part of the problem. The bigger issue deals with the way teachers themselves are trained. If the professional development center in which they are trained looks like a traditional school with classrooms and corridors and the pedagogies employed in their training is largely teacher-directed, why is it a surprise if these teachers go back to school, to their traditional

Figure 10-13: *Use of the outdoor areas for learning, eating and socializing is a big feature of GOGYA. Notice the lower level amphitheater seating for small outdoor gatherings. Exterior shading can be opened or closed depending on the time of day.*

Figure 10-14: *The authors with our smart and articulate young guides Arya Sharma and Shriyansh Suparkar at VEGA School in New Delhi, India.*

classrooms, and employ the same teacher-directed practices with their students?

Our answer to the above dilemma is to develop professional development centers where the curriculum, space and the pedagogy are all modern and contemporary. That means the minute a teacher walks into such a facility, they realize the space is like no school they have ever taught in. That's just the first step. The full potential of the innovative spaces they occupy during their training is realized when they learn in the exact same way we would want their students to learn. In other words, the professional development center itself is designed to function like a Learning Community, the training stresses collaboration and the work is mostly directed by the learners. With this kind of professional development, teachers will be well prepared to take full advantage of innovative learning spaces at their own schools while encouraging and facilitating a student-directed model of learning.

Figure 10-15: *Ask your child what they learned at school today and usually you will get a shrug. However, ask what they 'did' at school today and you will get a very enthusiastic account of the day's activities.*
Art at VEGA.

VEGA SCHOOL, NEW DELHI

Democracy in Action

On a bright winter day in 2017, authors Prakash and Roni visited VEGA School in New Delhi to take stock of their innovative facilities and learn about their unique educational model. We were greeted at reception and immediately introduced to Arya Sharma and Shriyansh Suparkar, two 9-year-old students who spent the next hour conducting us on a school tour. During the tour they explained the VEGA educational philosophy of project-based learning and also discussed some of their own community service assignments like campaigning for clean air (a critically important issue for New Delhi, a city that struggles with very high levels of air pollution) and building religious tolerance.

What struck us was these students' level of maturity and their complete confidence while answering our many questions. During the tour they also showed us their primary learning areas or "classroom" spaces. Designed with no walls, these spaces

10 CHAPTER NEW DIRECTIONS FOR A NEW WORLD

would hardly qualify as traditional classrooms. There were breakout areas everywhere and no corridors. There was an indoor gymnasium which also served as a multipurpose hall for music and dance and community events. The small outdoor space on the tight urban site was fully utilized for outdoor activities and greenery.

After we had parted company with our young hosts we were introduced to 9-year-old Netanya Saini who had a slightly different assignment of giving us an in-depth look at what education at VEGA looks like and what it seeks to accomplish. Students are treated like partners and participate in goal setting. They are introduced to the work they will be doing throughout the semester and given the tools to measure their own progress. Netanya made a formal presentation of her portfolio during which she showed us actual examples of her work and the progress she had made through the semester.

For example, she said she had started the year with the goal of becoming a better communicator — this made us smile because she had obviously met and exceeded this goal by a wide margin! Throughout her presentation, which took about 25 minutes, we interrupted her with questions wondering if she could be "rattled" but she remained calm and patiently answered

Figure 10-16: *A student at VEGA will be able to solve problems, communicate, reflect, be curious and creative, articulate, analyze, evaluate, and collaborate effectively.*
A Learning Community in Action at VEGA.

10 CHAPTER NEW DIRECTIONS FOR A NEW WORLD

Figure 10-17: *The Design for Change initiative that educational visionary Kiran Bir Sethi started as a humble experiment at Riverside, a small school she founded in Ahmedabad, India has, today, positively impacted the lives of 2.2 million children and 65,000 teachers in over 60 countries.*

us, again exhibiting a level of maturity that was way beyond her years. Naturally, our inclination was to believe that VEGA had chosen Netanya because she was their "ringer" and we asked her this question as well. She looked surprised by the question and said, "No. This is not something I do every day. All the students here are given turns presenting their work. Today just happened to be my turn."

Almost two hours had gone by before we met with the school leadership but those two hours told us that VEGA is not just talking the talk but making genuine attempts to walk the walk. We don't know too many schools that would trust their visitors to learn all about their school exclusively from students but VEGA does its best to practice what it preaches — that student voices are important. Sure, there are elements at VEGA that look very "school-like" and at least some of the content the students learn looks and feels like the stuff young kids are force-

> What started as a humble experiment at Riverside, a small school in Ahmedabad, India has, today, positively impacted the lives of 2.2 million children and 65,000 teachers in over 60 countries.

Figure 10-18: *At Riverside, no child is too young to have her voice heard.*

fed every day in schools throughout the world. The difference at VEGA is that the school is making a genuine attempt to help students develop the important soft skills of complex problem solving and critical thinking along with all the other ancillary skills like emotional intelligence and empathy. They also clearly understand that content is mostly there as a vehicle for skill building.

It is interesting to see the words used by VEGA to describe their own philosophy because these words are very much in line with the fundamental thesis of this book. In their own words: "You will be amazed with this little experiment! Ask your child what they learned at school today and usually you will get a shrug. However, ask what they 'did' at school today and you will get a very enthusiastic account of the day's activities. Top schools worldwide are aware that children do not go to school to learn; they go because they have fun doing interesting activities with their friends. Vega Schools' curriculum takes this into account and draws on the best practises utilised by schools across the globe to interweave learning into what children love doing. As a result, a student at VEGA will be able to solve problems, communicate, reflect, be curious and creative, articulate, analyze, evaluate, and collaborate effectively. Success breeds confidence, helping children develop lifelong skills."[83]

---

[83] Immersive Learning. VEGA School. https://www.vega.edu.in/immersive-learning

Figure 10-19: *The Riverside campus is designed to feel warm and welcoming and not intimidating and institutional like most school buildings.*

10 CHAPTER NEW DIRECTIONS FOR A NEW WORLD

VEGA is the brainchild of Sandy Hooda "whose life mission is to revolutionise education based on research on 'why' and 'how' we learn so there is perfect harmony between school education, love of learning, and success in life."[84]

I CAN — THE RIVERSIDE STORY
Kiran Bir Sethi and the Importance of Leadership

Even as Barack Obama was making *Yes We Can* a national anthem, a similar refrain, *I CAN*, was already taking education by storm empowering tens of thousands of children across the world to contribute the best of themselves. In a startling departure from the prevailing education model where children powerlessly jump through predictable hoops, the *I CAN* movement gave

Figure 10-20: *Outdoor learning is a key component of the curriculum at Riverside.*

---

[84] https://www.vega.edu.in/board-and-mentors

10 CHAPTER NEW DIRECTIONS FOR A NEW WORLD

Figure 10-21: *Kiran Bir Sethi with Pope Francis.*

each child a voice, harnessed his or her passion and directed it toward making positive change in the world. What started as a humble experiment at Riverside, a small school in Ahmedabad, India has, today, positively impacted the lives of 2.2 million children and 65,000 teachers in over 60 countries.

It all started in 2001 with one parent, Kiran Bir Sethi, realizing an obvious truth about education after observing the experience of her own son — that it doesn't work! She was shocked not just by how education was, quite literally, robbing her child of his voice and creativity but also saddened by how much it was impacting her own behavior toward him as a parent.

While Kiran had no experience as an educator, her training as an interior designer became the basis for crafting a whole new educational model which she brought to life when she founded Riverside School. As an outsider with no particular ties to education or its entrenched interests, Kiran started with the child, the ostensible "user," whose welfare the education establishment seemed to have completely abandoned. Instead of taking her cues from the so-called "successful" schools around the country, Kiran decided to go her own way. Riverside, she decided, would be founded on these three basic values that would go on to become the cornerstones of the teaching and learning model at the school:

1. Be Humane
2. Have Empathy
3. Be Ethical

Riverside combines these very human ideals with the three tenets of design thinking which are Inspiration, Ideation and Implementation.[85] *I CAN* was in place at Riverside as a philosophical driver but it became a national and global movement as an offshoot of the **Design for Change** initiative begun by Kiran Bir Sethi in 2009 which brings all these ideas and principles under one roof and makes them easily accessible and available to schools everywhere.

Just as Kiran did with Riverside itself, the children who are *I CAN* advocates start every endeavor with the WHO and WHY which leads them to the WHAT and HOW in finding solutions to social and community problems. Contrast this with traditional school curriculums that are, almost exclusively, about the what and how. *I CAN* is "based on a simple but revolutionary model: It asks kids to *feel* any problem that bothers them, *imagine* a way to make it better, *do* an act of change, and *share* their story of change with the world."[86]

Feel, Imagine, Do and Share. Four simple words that translate into one of the most powerful curriculums in the world imbued with the potential to deliver all the content and skills that children will need to grow up as confident, responsible, creative and contributing members of society. Motivated by their own interests and passion and driven by the high ideal of improving the world, children are naturally driven to excel. This push for excellence doesn't end with any particular achievement but is rather a *growth mindset*[87] that encourages evolutionary thinking.

The obvious question on most parents' minds, even those who are inclined to fully agree with the foundational underpinnings of the Riverside model, would be one of student performance on traditional measures like test scores and college admissions. For those who understand the essence of real learning, spelled out eloquently by Richard Elmore in Part Two of this book, it should come as no surprise that Riverside is consistently among a small handful of the most successful schools in India when it comes to such traditional academic achievement measures. As we have noted throughout this book, real, authentic and deep learning is more likely to happen when it becomes a natural, collateral benefit of activities that students are truly engaged in. Riverside is a perfect example of this principle in action.

For her outstanding work as an educator, Kiran was featured in an inspiring TED talk in 2010.[88] She went on to win the coveted Index **Design to Improve Life Award**, the Rockefeller Foundation **Youth Innovation Award**, **Patricia Blunt Koldyke Fellowship** from the Chicago Council on Global Affairs, **Asia Game Changer** award, and the **Excellence in Instructional Leadership** Award. These awards do not come close to listing all of her accomplishments and international recognitions. Most ordinary people would be satisfied with this impressive resume but for Kiran, this has been just a springboard to her next big adventure on behalf of children. "On 9th June, 2018 she met the Pope in the Vatican to sign an Agreement whereby DFC is being introduced in over 460,000 Catholic Schools across the Globe"[89] and in 2019 Kiran is organizing the *I CAN* Global Summit in Rome for 4,000 children from 100 countries.

---

[85] Brown, T. 2008. Design Thinking. Harvard Business Review
[86] Asia Game Changer Awards. https://asiasociety.org/asia-game-changers/kiran-bir-sethi
[87] Mindset: The New Psychology of Success Paperback – December 26, 2007 by Carol S. Dweck
[88] Kids Take Charge. TED TALK 2009
https://www.ted.com/talks/kiran_bir_sethi_teaches_kids_to_take_charge?language=en
[89] Speaker Profile, World Government Summit, Dubai, UAE

10 CHAPTER NEW DIRECTIONS FOR A NEW WORLD

The obvious moral of this story about Kiran Bir Sethi and Riverside School is the importance of leadership to usher in real, lasting and enduring change in education. Of course we recognize that not everyone can be a Kiran but there is no reason each one of us can't add our own stories to the *I CAN* movement just as millions of previously invisible children have been doing for a decade. All of us interested to see education fulfil its promise of becoming the leveler of the playing field so that every child has a real opportunity to succeed in life can take a page out of Kiran's book and become agents for change by first working within and then slowly expanding our own sphere of influence to leave a positive imprint on the world.

PART II
THE CHALLENGES OF LEARNING AND DESIGN

Richard F. Elmore, Professor Emeritus

Harvard University

CHAPTER 11
THE CHALLENGES OF LEARNING AND DESIGN

Richard F. Elmore[1]

[Learning organizations are] organizations where people continually expand their capacity to create the results they truly desire, where new and expansive patterns of thinking are nurtured, where collective aspiration is set free, and where people are continually learning to see the whole together. (Senge, 1990/2006, 3)

Suppose, for a moment, that we were asked to design an organization that would enable adults and young people to develop and exercise their capabilities as learners — nothing more complicated than that. In other words, suppose we were asked to design a learning organization. Suppose also that this organization was an embodiment, at the collective level, of what a healthy, engaged learner would look like at the individual level. That is, it would be an organization in more or less constant engagement with its environment, capable of more or less continuous adaptation in concert with its surroundings, and more or less agile and flexible in its ability to adapt its internal structures and processes to what it learns through this engagement. In other words, this learning organization would look and behave like a highly evolved learning organism, constantly adapting and changing in response to its collective aspirations and its capabilities as a learner.

A major premise of this book is that the physical environments in which we learn should reflect our most powerful aspirations and our most promising ideas about learning. A corollary of this premise is that our most powerful ideas about how learning occurs are constantly changing in response to new knowledge and our experience adapting our learning practices to the practical demands of daily work. In an ideal world, schools and the systems in which they are embedded would model for the rest of society what learning should look like. In the real world, schools often model what learning used to look like in a world that no longer exists. What would it look like if schools, as intentional learning environments, actually became "learning organizations" in the sense defined above? They would not just be places where adults and children engaged in predictable patterns of activity grounded in past practice; they would be places where the very definition of what learning is, and how it is enacted,

> **What would it look like if schools, as intentional learning environments, actually became "learning organizations"?**

11 CHAPTER THE CHALLENGES OF LEARNING AND DESIGN

are themselves the result of constant learning — from research, from experience, from observation, from aspirations, and, possibly, from wondering: wondering whether we are ambitious enough in our understanding of learning as a human activity.

In this chapter, I will ask my readers initially to consider five propositions about what it means to treat schools, and a number of other learning environments, as learning organizations. I will then offer a framework for analyzing a range of ways in which learning occurs, and the organizational structures and processes underlying those learning modalities. Finally, I will offer a set of preliminary design principles, drawn from current research on learning, that can inform the practices of building and sustaining learning organizations. I conclude with a set of challenges for the future design of learning environments.

> They would be places where the very definition of what learning is, and how it is enacted, are themselves the result of constant learning — from research, from experience, from observation, from aspirations.

FIVE PROPOSITIONS

To be clear, "learning" in the context of this chapter, is the ability of humans to consciously modify beliefs, understandings, and actions in the presence of evidence, experience, and reflection. A later section of this chapter expands on this definition. For the moment, it is sufficient to observe that, according to this definition, learning is an activity that humans pursue out of evolutionary, biological, and practical necessity. "Design" means the intentional use of cultural, behavioral, and physical norms and structures to achieve a desirable result, individually and collectively. Learning is central to the evolution and survival of the human species. Design is the means by which humans intentionally create various means and modes of learning.

FIVE PROPOSITIONS ABOUT LEARNING AND DESIGN

1. Understand and appreciate how the existing design of schools reflects present and past theories of learning.

The daily demands of work in schools are not necessarily conducive to reflection on organizational design. More likely, people learn to adapt to the structures and processes they are given, at most making marginal adaptations to accommodate individual differences and preferences in practice. For most educators, the design of learning spaces is not the result of conscious action, but a "given," in the same sense that the water in an aquarium is for the fish that swim in it.

In fact, the existing design of schools is the accumulated residue of thousands of choices, deliberate or not, over decades of daily work. The cellular structure of classrooms, for example, embodies a theory that learning should occur in a physical setting in which an adult typically supervises a group of students for a particular period of time. The array of classrooms along hallways is a way of managing and controlling the movement of students in more or less predictable ways through the course of the day — embodying an explicit theory of custody and control in a physical environment. The presence, or absence, of dedicated workspace for adults, individually or collectively, embodies a theory of how adults interact, or not, with each other and around their work with students. The degree to which teachers "own" the space they teach in, and treat it as their personal preserve, represents a complex set of agreements over the private use of public space. The separation of administrative functions

11 CHAPTER THE CHALLENGES OF LEARNING AND DESIGN

11 CHAPTER THE CHALLENGES OF LEARNING AND DESIGN

in dedicated spaces embodies a theory about the division of work between those who work directly with students and those who supervise that work — a division that separates learning work from administrative work, spatially and culturally. The physical arrangement of space within classrooms, and the variability among classrooms in how space is used, communicates how adults think about learning and how the organization as a whole treats individual and collective theories of learning. The fact that these theories underlying the design of schools may have receded into a fog of unconsciousness for people who work in schools does not mean that they aren't powerful determinants of how we define and enact learning.

The first step in understanding the relationship between learning and design is to treat familiar patterns of organization and practice as default theories of learning. They exist because they represented, at some point in time, a defensible theory of

Figure 11-1: *The structure of the environment constrains, shapes, and represents the learning that occurs within it. For example, the stepped seating adjacent to the Meadowlark School cafeteria allows this space to double as a presentation and performance space. Unlike most school cafeterias that are used only for lunch, spaces like this can be used throughout the school day for small group work, messy projects, and independent study.*
Photo © Fred J. Fuhrmeister.

11 CHAPTER THE CHALLENGES OF LEARNING AND DESIGN

Figure 11-2: *Contrast this image with the image of a traditional classroom shown in Figure 11-3. Those who designed this space obviously had a different philosophy about custody and control.*
Learning Community at Fisher STEAM Middle School, Greenville, South Carolina.
Photo by Kris Decker/Firewater Photography.

11 CHAPTER THE CHALLENGES OF LEARNING AND DESIGN

learning. There is no such thing as a "neutral" learning environment — a physical and cultural space that can accommodate any conceivable theory of learning. The fact that the environment is familiar does not make it functional as a learning environment. Not all theories of learning are adaptable to all physical environments, and vice versa. The structure of the environment constrains, shapes, and represents the definition of learning that occurs within it. [2]

2. The deliberate design of learning environments requires a reversal of the traditional relationship between learning and schooling.

The conventional way that educators have thought about the relationship between learning and schooling is to ask how our best ideas about learning can be made to fit within an existing cultural, physical, and organizational model. "Innovation" in schooling is typically conceived as changing practices within an established, fixed form of organization, or at most making marginal adaptations within a fixed physical and organizational structure to accommodate incremental changes in learning. Deliberate design requires starting from a set of principles — a theory of learning — derived from research, reflection on practice, aspirations, and action-forcing questions, then creating structures and processes that accommodate those principles. In conventional innovation, learning adapts to schooling; in deliberate design, learning precedes and informs structures and processes that enable learning (Elmore 2018 and Ellis, Goodyear and Marmot 2018a and b).

It is one thing to state this proposition, and quite another to enact it. In advanced

11 CHAPTER THE CHALLENGES OF LEARNING AND DESIGN

> Learning is the ability of humans to consciously modify beliefs, understandings, and actions in the presence of evidence, experience, and reflection.

societies, education is a heavily institutionalized sector, which means that the structures and processes by which the sector is governed and administered carry with them a particular mindset that values predictability and stability. Furthermore, the physical and cultural constraints on learning represent heavily institutionalized interests, ranging from local governance structures to organized interest groups to commercial interests to powerful political interests. A shift to deliberate design requires a shift in mindset, from predictability and stability to informed choice and adaptation, from established patterns and procedures to flexibility and responsiveness, from established "truths" to inquiry and questions.

Deliberate design often involves, as we shall see, a painful reckoning with the difference between the espoused and enacted beliefs that characterize institutions. Specifically, schools may be idealized in institutional rhetoric as places where learning occurs when, in fact, their primary social function may be the allocation of privilege in society.

3. Multiple modes of learning require multiple modes of practice and multiple modes of organization.

As we shall see later, learning is a basic human activity that occurs naturally in many forms, individually and collectively, throughout society (National Research Council 2000). Schooling, on the other hand, is a particular, institutionalized form of learning that occurs in an institutionally defined sector, with its own structural and procedural imperatives. Human beings have come to embody, through evolution and practice, multiple modes of learning, some of which can be accommodated in formal institutions and others that require modes of interaction that are much more fluid and loosely distributed.

The deliberate design of learning environments requires an understanding of the full range of modalities of learning, not just the familiar, established modalities. Powerful design is expansive rather than exclusive in its focus, accommodating the full range of ways in which humans engage in deliberate learning. Design is about expanding rather than containing learning, opening access rather than controlling access, adapting to differences in learning modalities and preferences, rather than restricting modalities and controlling preferences.

Again, this shift is as much, or more, a shift in mindset as it is a shift in technical or managerial practice. A design mindset carries with it a different, broader vocabulary of alternative forms for organizing learning, coupled with a deeper appreciation of the breadth of human capabilities for learning and for exporting opportunities to learn in a broader, more diverse human environment.

4. Our knowledge of learning itself is changing as our ideas about how to organize learning are changing; different contexts require different solutions to common problems.

Conventional ideas about "innovation" in schooling embody what might be called an "implementation"

> Design is about expanding rather than containing learning, opening access rather than controlling access, adapting to differences in learning modalities and preferences, rather than restricting modalities and controlling preferences.

Figure 11-3: *The fact that classroom spaces like this are familiar and commonplace is no reason to assume that they are functional learning environments.*

mindset, where a new idea about learning becomes embodied in a particular set of practices, and those practices are implemented in schools and classrooms. The idea of implementation carries with it the requirement of fidelity to the original practice and the notion that "successful" innovations are ones that can be implemented "at scale." Good innovations are ones that can produce more or less identical replicates in multiple locations across different social and cultural contexts.

As our knowledge of learning increases, the implementation mindset becomes less and less useful. Despite our best efforts, our best ideas produce highly variable results in different contexts, depending on the capabilities, preferences, and conditions under which real people try to adapt them. At the same time, research on the neuroscience of learning, as we shall see, is leading away from the expectation that standardized responses to individual learning differences will produce robust results. We are living through a period in which the basic science of learning at the individual level is growing at a fast pace and our understandings of differences among individuals and between individuals and the context in which they learn are increasing. While the implementation mindset might be a convenient fiction for a highly institutionalized sector, like education, it is an increasingly limited mindset for thinking about learning (Honig, ed. 2006).

Robust designs for learning in this context are ones that deliberately design for change and uncertainty, for contingency and adaptability to specific individual and contextual differences, for questions rather than answers, for curiosity and wonder rather than settled assumptions and conventional wisdom. In other words, robust designs are designs that enable deliberate learning over time in the face of changing knowledge, rather than implementing solutions to past problems.

> Despite our best efforts, our best ideas produce highly variable results in different contexts, depending on the capabilities, preferences, and conditions under which real people try to adapt them. At the same time, research on the neuroscience of learning is leading away from the expectation that standardized responses to individual learning differences will produce robust results.

5. Metaphors matter.

We have known for decades, thanks to the work of cognitive psychologists and neuroscientists, that human beings rely heavily on metaphors to make sense of the difficult and tangled realities of daily life and problem solving (Lakoff and Johnson 1980/2003). Metaphors have many functions, but among the most important is their ability to make deliberate, symbolic simplifications of complex problems, and to make those simplifications available as guides to understanding and action. Metaphorical thinking is deeply embedded in the language we use to make sense of our lives: "that music left me floating on air," "I left the meeting feeling like the rug had been pulled out from under me," "garbage in, garbage out," etc. Metaphors can be useful in helping to ease the transition from a stable, predictable environment to a more uncertain, less predictable environment in which opportunities for learning will abound, but safety and security are less available.

Let me propose one possible metaphor for the situation in which we currently find ourselves around the conceptualization and design of new learning environments. The metaphor derives from the physics of changes in the state of matter. In the physical world, we experience solid things (the table on which my computer is sitting); liquid things (the coffee in the cup on the table); and gaseous things (the air that is circulating through the room) as distinctive states of matter. We are comfortable with these distinctions in everyday life because they behave predictably and we don't have to spend a lot of time worrying about whether they will change at random — the table will probably still be there tomorrow morning when I wake up.

For a physicist, however, this stable, predictable world is a boring illusion. What the physicist sees is a world that is constantly in flux, in which changes in the state of matter are occurring all the time in various forms in response to various changes in conditions. Highly elaborate crystalline structures turn into amorphous fluids that, in turn, transform into gases, all with the addition or subtraction of energy. The physical world is full of a massive number of these transformations, each one unique in the form and nature of the transformation, each one worthy of detailed description and study, each process leading to a new set

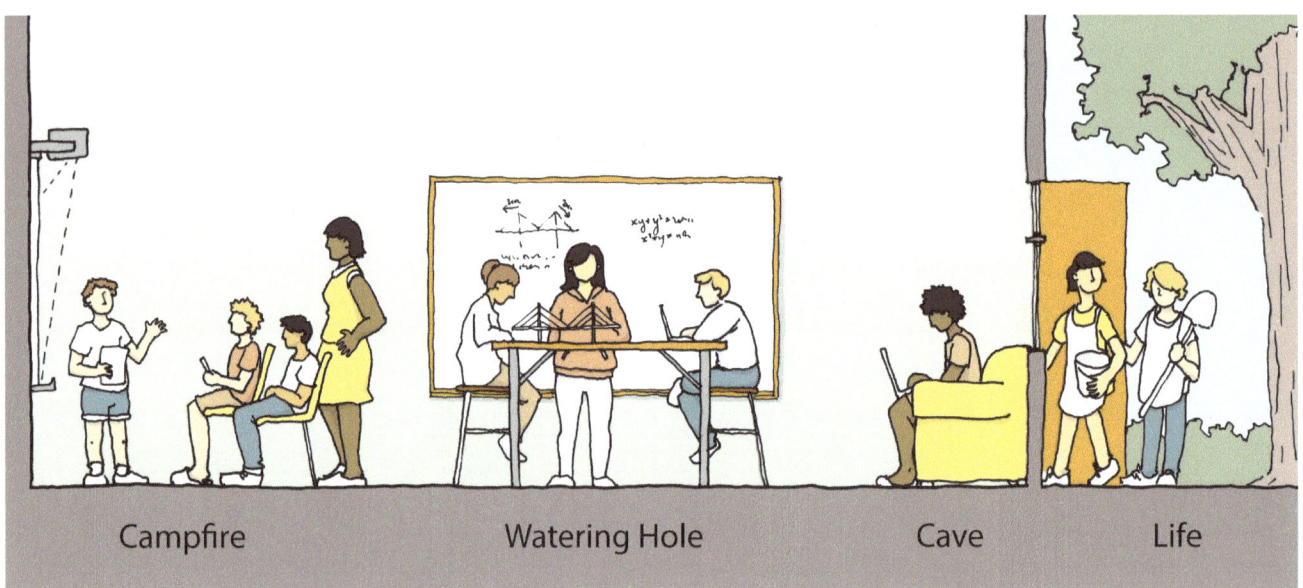

Figure 11-4: *The deliberate design of learning environments requires an understanding of the full range of modalities of learning, not just the familiar, established modalities. Classroom-based schools are optimized for Campfire learning but don't do as well with the other modalities.*
This diagram shows Dr. David Thornburg's four "primordial learning metaphors."

of questions about the subtleties and differences among different types of transformations. [3]

One could think about the transformation of learning in society in a similar way. As an advanced economy and society, we have come to associate learning with a stable, enduring crystalline institutional structure that is more or less comprehensible to those who inhabit it and that embeds a metaphor in our minds that (we think) helps make sense of how a certain part of the world works, and relieves us of the more complex task of understanding how learning actually works as an individual and social activity.

> With a relatively modest shift in metaphors, from a stable crystalline structure to a continuum of states of matter from the stable, to the malleable, to the atmospheric, we would see learning in an entirely different light. We would see it as a naturally occurring human activity, driven by biological and evolutionary imperatives.

But with a relatively modest shift in metaphors, from a stable crystalline structure to a continuum of states of matter from the stable, to the malleable, to the atmospheric, we would see learning in an entirely different light. We would see it as a naturally occurring human activity, driven by biological and evolutionary imperatives, that can — and will — take an infinite variety of forms, some of which we can deliberately shape to specific human ends, if we understand them. We can choose, first, not to be constrained by one particular state of matter, and second, to exercise human control and agency to shape new organizational forms that capitalize on the natural variation in states of learning.

In the following section, I will lay out a simple framework that accomplishes a couple of purposes. It helps describe the familiar, highly institutionalized forms of learning, but it does so in a way that, I hope, makes the familiar look and feel a bit strange. Making the familiar strange is an important step, I think, in "unfreezing" the crystalline structure of institutionalized learning and beginning to imagine more agile and fluid organizational forms. Another purpose of the framework is to begin (and here I stress begin) to capture other forms of learning that are abroad in society and to suggest how they might be incorporated into our thinking about the design of learning environments for the future.

A FOUR-FOLD FRAMEWORK [4]

First the simplicity, then the complexity. The archetypal four-fold table is a way of incorporating a modest degree of complexity into a relatively simple model. To do so, however, requires some deliberate oversimplification, which we'll have to adjust for later.

The simple version goes as follows: You can think of the social organization of learning along two broad dimensions: (1) the degree to which learning is organized hierarchically or in a more distributed, lateral way; and (2) the degree to which we think of learning as a primarily individual activity versus a more collective, social activity. *Hierarchy*, in this model, has a couple of meanings: it captures that sense in which learning is considered to consist mainly of the transfer of knowledge from one who is assumed to have it to one who doesn't; it also captures a form of organization of learning in which there are differences in status and authority between those who have knowledge and those who don't (yet, at least). *Distributed*, in this model, captures the idea that knowledge is not contained in any one place or institutional structure. It is, instead, available in a variety of different forms and from a variety of different sources, some through human interaction, some through various social artifacts. *Individual*, in this model, focuses on the motivations, actions, and choices of the individual as determinants of learning. *Collective* focuses on learning as an activity resulting from various forms of social interaction.

Each quadrant can be characterized as an "ideal type," an example that characterizes its essential characteristics. The upper left quadrant can be thought of as the classic comprehensive middle or high school. It is hierarchically organized in the sense that it typically entails traditional administration-teacher, teacher-student relations. It is primarily individually competitive in the sense that students are judged individually according to their academic performance by traditional measures. The learning model here is essentially one of knowledge transfer: information organized around a structured curriculum that is transferred from teachers to students and becomes knowledge by assimilation (or not). Success in this model is judged by attainment — the accumulation of course credits, grades, and test scores. This accumulation is thought to embody society's definition of "merit." That is, people who accumulate more of the valued indexes are thought to be "better" and "more deserving" of status than those who don't.

> The authority of schools in the leftward quadrants stems from two important sources. The first is the power of the state to compel participation of children in schooling — what I will call "custody and control." The second is the power of educational institutions at multiple levels to determine what constitutes valuable learning and the rewards that accrue to that learning.

The lower left quadrant is the more "progressive" version of the upper left. It still embodies the traditional adult-student, administration-teacher relationships, in the sense that the organization works primarily as a hierarchy of status and position, and knowledge is assumed to flow from adult to students in a structured way. The distinctive difference between the upper and lower left quadrants is that the upper left is an individually competitive model, where the purpose of schooling is to make distinctions among students based on various measures of academic "merit," whereas the lower left quadrant emphasizes socialization to a set of collective social norms, based on an adult's vision of a "good" society. Learning in this model is equally about meeting adult expectations for academic performance and demonstrating social values in student behavior. The ideal type in this quadrant might be John Dewey's vision of schooling as preparation for democratic citizenship, or, alternatively, a school founded and run by a religious community.

The important distinction here is that the leftward quadrants embody society's vision of what educational sociologists have called "real school" — organizations with hard physical boundaries in which adults and children engage in purposeful, structured activities, and learning is valued for its contribution to socially approved academic, economic, social, and cultural norms. These values and norms are quite literally transferred from adults to students, by teachers who claim their authority by appealing to governmental bodies or other organized collectivities. Learning, in this domain, can only occur as a result of an activity called teaching, and teaching must involve authoritative judgments of students, based on the values of the organization. Those authoritative judgments are thought to embody society's definitions of merit.

The authority of schools in the leftward quadrants stems from two important sources. The first is the power of the state to compel participation of children in schooling — what I will call "custody and control." The second is the power of educational institutions at multiple levels to determine what constitutes valuable learning and the rewards that accrue to that learning — what I will call "attainment." These sources of authority run deep in the social order of advanced societies. It is, for example, difficult for most adults to imagine something called "learning" happening in any fruitful way outside the boundaries of something called a school, despite the fact that the vast majority of what people learn does not occur in school. It is difficult for society as a whole to imagine a world in which children are not under the custody and control of an institution called school for something in the neighborhood of 16,000 hours of their prime years of development — even though most of the developmental

11 CHAPTER THE CHALLENGES OF LEARNING AND DESIGN

MODES OF LEARNING

Hierarchical Individual

Distributed Individual

Hierarchical Collective

Distributed Collective

Figure 11-5: *Modes of Learning.*

171

> Shifting from the leftward to the rightward quadrants involves shifting from a view of learning in which the value of knowledge is not mediated by authoritative institutions to one in which value is determined by its utility and meaning, broadly defined, to the learner.

growth that children experience occurs before they enter school and outside school after they enter. The leftward quadrants exercise enormous influence and control over society's understanding of learning.

Shifting from the left quadrants to the right quadrants means crossing a boundary that is unfamiliar in most discussions of organized learning but often quite familiar in terms of what people actually experience as learners. When I do clinical work with educators on learning, I often ask them to identify the most powerful learning experience they have had in the last six months or a year and to describe it in detail. The first few times I did this I was shocked by the results, but I have now come to accept the dominant pattern. The overwhelming pattern of responses is that adults describe very powerful, often transformational, learning experiences that have nothing to do with any formal organizational structure, much less their own schools. They describe things like physical and cognitive transformations necessary to master a musical instrument in midlife, the deep impacts of caring for an elderly parent or a disabled sibling on their identities and interpersonal skills, the shift in consciousness required to master an unfamiliar cuisine, the curious reorganization of the cognitive and somatic parts of the body involved in trying to do yoga, etc. When we debrief these discussions two important themes typically emerge: these experiences are "powerful" because they require people to exercise agency and control over something in their lives that has meaning to them; and these experiences are deeply individual, involving choices and values that are often outside the familiar routines and relationships in their daily lives.

Shifting from the leftward to the rightward quadrants involves shifting from a view of learning in which the value of knowledge is not mediated by authoritative institutions to one in which value is determined by its utility and meaning, broadly defined, to the learner. In this model, when we say that learning is "distributed," rather than hierarchical, we mean that agency and control over what is learned shifts in important ways from institutions to learners. The upper right quadrant is the most extreme form of distributed learning, in which the learner decides what learning has value in a highly individualized way and sets about acquiring knowledge through whatever modalities he or she chooses. The range of learning modalities is determined by a combination of opportunity and preference, all under the learner's control — books, articles, online text and video resources, lectures, individual tutorials, casual group discussions, peer-to-peer relations, etc. The actual modalities of learning in this quadrant are less important than the skills required to exercise agency, choice, and judgment in the purpose of learning and the evaluation of sources. It is tempting to think of the ideal type in this quadrant as the archetypal nerd in sweatpants and hoodie sitting in front of a computer, oblivious to the world at large. In fact, the growth of learning in the digital space has accelerated the growth of individually driven learning immensely. Driven by flexibility of format and rules of engagement, the demand for learning tailored to individual utility and preference has become the norm in the digital learning space. If you are struggling with factoring quadratic equations in your middle school algebra class, not only do you now have the option of learning the operations online, unconstrained by the time, personnel, and physical space of schools,

> Driven by flexibility of format and rules of engagement, the demand for learning tailored to individual utility and preference has become the norm in the digital learning space.

EXHIBIT 1: MODES OF LEARNING FRAMEWORK

HIERARCHICAL / INDIVIDUAL
- Social agreement on what should be learned...
- Embodied in texts, standards, outcome measures
- Individual learning evaluated based on common metrics, relative to standards and in relation to others
- "Merit" defined by performance and attainment
- The consequences that follow from individual choices are the individual's responsibility

DISTRIBUTED / INDIVIDUAL
- Learning is a human, biological imperative that occurs with or without formal teaching or schooling
- Individuals ultimately decide what types of learning matter most to them...
- According to their own needs, aptitudes, and interests
- Sources of learning are widely distributed in society, and boundaries around sources are diffuse and permeable
- Goals of learning are individually determined; what learning is "good" for the individual cannot be collectively determined

HIERARCHICAL / COLLECTIVE
- Institutions embody society's collective goals
- Decisions about what should be learned are embodied in the rules, structures, and processes of these institutions
- The primary function of learning in schools is to socialize individuals to a common body of content and social norms
- Society exercises its collective responsibility toward individuals through organized learning

DISTRIBUTED / COLLECTIVE
- Learning as a social process is embedded in consensual communities, organized in networks
- Over time, individuals choose the communities with which they affiliate...
- According to their needs, aptitudes, and interests
- Society promotes learning through the networks

Figure 11-6: *Modes of Learning Framework.*

but you can choose which platforms and modalities best adapt to your learning needs. Furthermore, there is no prescribed curriculum structure to tell you that it is "inappropriate" to drop into a lesson on differential calculus until you have successfully taken and "passed" a battery of prerequisite courses. If you are interested in the mathematics of acceleration or how to compute the area under a curve, you can find somewhere to learn it in a couple of keystrokes.

The lower right quadrant takes us into the distributed/collective world of voluntary communities of learners, joined in various degrees of loose and tight networking around domains of knowledge in which individuals share a mutual interest. In the upper right quadrant, networking as a form of organization is implicit in the technology. In the lower right quadrant, networking is in the foreground as the dominant form of social interaction around knowledge. Working with schools and teachers in the dusty agricultural Central Valley of California, I discovered that the dominant form of organized learning for adolescents and college undergraduates was what I came to call the "Starbucks Circle." I would routinely walk into a local Starbucks in the early morning hours or the midafternoon and see groups of largely Latino students sitting in homework circles (yes, teachers, they actually do share their homework), and study groups loosely organized but deeply engaged in learning. It was clear from my conversations with

> The leftward quadrants embody society's vision of what educational sociologists have called "real school"— organizations with hard physical boundaries in which adults and children engage in purposeful, structured activities, and learning is valued for its contribution to socially-approved academic, economic, social, and cultural norms.

them that they viewed this form of organization as a survival mechanism in a world they perceived as largely indifferent to their needs as learners. The variety of networked learning communities is infinite, largely due to the flexibility of networked structures in accommodating diverse interests and levels of engagement. The important contrast here with hierarchical forms of learning is that networks can accommodate vastly different levels of expertise in areas of common interest so that the flow of knowledge among participants is very fluid and efficient. People can find others in the network with a command of knowledge close enough to their individual zone of proximal development so that they can learn something of value without having to go to a single source.

The lower right quadrant is now the dominant form of learning and knowledge transmission in advanced research and development fields. Most university professors, professional practitioners, research and development experts, and entrepreneurs operate in highly networked environments where their success depends on their ability to build relationships of mutual benefit across domains of knowledge and levels of expertise. The kind of learning required to master these skills cannot be contained in conventional forms of organization. It can, however, be learned through sustained engagement and practice, through the development and use of agency and choice, and through the cultivation of insight and creativity. One has only to look at the design of physical and digital space surrounding major research universities to see this model in action. Private companies' research labs are located cheek by jowl with university labs organized around transportation and communication hubs, all linked globally through high-speed digital environments working 24-7 on the transfer of information among nodes in complex networks.

As noted above, any schematic model compromises the true complexity of learning as an individual and social activity. But there are ways in which this schematic helps us understand important design decisions. One way it helps is to reinforce the idea that design decisions have real consequences for the development and growth of human beings as learners. By design decisions I mean choices about which modalities of learning are important to cultivate and nurture and which physical, organizational, social, and cultural affordances go with which modalities of learning. My experience working with educators is that they tend to think that any modality of learning can be

> The overwhelming pattern of responses is that adults describe very powerful, often transformational, learning experiences that have nothing to do with any formal organizational structure, much less their own schools.

Figure 11-7: *When we say that learning is "distributed," rather than hierarchical, we mean that agency and control over what is learned shifts in important ways from institutions to learners. Rendering of the performance commons at the new secondary school for the Yew Chung International School of Chongqing.*

made to fit into any standard form of school organization, but the evidence shows this is clearly not true. Let me illustrate: "blended learning" is now a popular adaptation of technology to conventional schooling. Advocates of blended learning think it is a major innovation. In most instances, what blended learning means is that students engage course material online before or after class time, typically in lecture form, so that class time can be used for less structured, more discussion-oriented learning. In terms of the Modes of Learning framework, this version of blended learning is not really very innovative at all. First of all, the whole activity is embedded in a hierarchically determined structure of control and attainment, so that choice and agency on the part of the learner occurs, if at all, in a carefully scripted setting. Second, the technology is used to reinforce a hierarchical modality of learning (knowledge flows from the teacher to the student); the only thing that has changed is the means of transmission, from lecture to video clip. Third, the modality of learning actually increases adult control over student choices by requiring students to engage a larger share of their discretionary time in adult-controlled activity. These features may be regarded positively in a hierarchical learning environment, but they are hardly "innovative" in a broader framework that sees the individual learner as the central agent in learning and development. Design decisions have real consequences for learning, whether they reinforce existing modalities or disrupt them. Often we confuse any kind of change with changes in learning, when most "change" is designed to reinforce existing modalities of learning.

Another useful contribution of the framework is to provide a clearer way of differentiating learning, as an individual and social activity that occurs in society at large, from schooling, which, at least in its existing form, is a highly institutionalized form of learning. The big design questions for the future will

> The important contrast here with hierarchical forms of learning is that networks can accommodate vastly different levels of expertise in areas of common interest so that the flow of knowledge among participants is very fluid and efficient.

revolve around the relationship between schooling and the broader, more extensive, increasingly fluid and responsive learning sector. These will not be easy questions to answer, much less to translate into useful, functional, inspiring physical designs for learning environments. One way into these questions is to take a provisional look at the future of learning through the lens of current research on the neuroscience of learning.

THE FUTURE OF LEARNING

> One whole line of empirical research on memory and learning involves the productive role that forgetting plays in the learning process, as it introduces pauses to revisit and reconcile earlier understandings and misconceptions, and results in "interleaving" of prior and subsequent learning with earlier memories.

Learning is the ability to consciously modify beliefs, understandings, and actions in the presence of evidence, experience, and reflection. [5]

We live in a world in which learning is largely defined by institutions and the organized interests these institutions represent. We are emerging into a world in which learning, as a human activity, is increasingly escaping the bounds of institutions, and in which the stakes for individuals and for society at large increasingly depend on our ability to understand the many forms and modalities of learning and to create access to those forms through the use of design. The future of learning for society as a whole depends on our ability to disentangle our understandings of learning from its institutional constraints and to imagine a future in which designs for learning follow and enhance the actual contours of human capabilities.

The definition of learning above collapses a vast welter of theory and research, and, of necessity, leaves out much of the conflict and disagreement over the meaning of learning that has occurred historically. It does, however, reflect a view of learning that represents the current convergence of thought among behavioral psychologists and students of the neuroscience of learning.

One way to understand the significance of this definition is to say what it does not include — that is, what learning is not. Primarily, and most controversially, in this definition learning is not memory, in the usual colloquial sense of that term. Memory is an important cognitive process by which knowledge and experience are encoded and stored for later use, but learning is not synonymous with the capacity to remember things. The reasons for this distinction run deep in theory and research, but the simplified version is that it turns out that memory — the ability to remember and repeat things experienced in the past — is a very unreliable proxy for actually knowing things. Memory, it turns out, is not just the storage and retrieval of facts and experience. Memory is a jumble of initial experience, combined with and corrupted by all subsequent recall, new information and experience related to the initial experience, continuously revised by all future experience. Memory plays a role in learning; memory is not, itself, a reliable proxy for learning (Schacter 2001, Kandel 2006). Indeed, one whole line of empirical research on memory and learning involves the productive role that forgetting plays

> Memory is an important cognitive process by which knowledge and experience are encoded and stored for later use, but learning is not synonymous with the capacity to remember things. The reasons for this distinction run deep in theory and research.

11 CHAPTER THE CHALLENGES OF LEARNING AND DESIGN

in the learning process, as it introduces pauses to revisit and reconcile earlier understandings and misconceptions, and results in "interleaving" of prior and subsequent learning with earlier memories. [6]

Nor is memory a unitary phenomenon. Long-term memory, the most unreliable form of memory, is quite distinct from working memory, which might be thought of as the just-in-time workhorse of active learning. Judy Willis, a clinical neurologist who also became a classroom teacher, gives the most lucid account of how memory works as an

> For Information to make its way through working memory into long-term memory, it needs to find a place in an existing neural network that, in effect, creates meaning for the learner. That is, it has to have some correspondence to some prior knowledge or experience.

aid to learning. For Information to make its way through working memory into long-term memory, it needs to find a place in an existing neural network that, in effect, creates meaning for the learner. That is, it has to have some correspondence to some prior knowledge or experience (no matter how unreliable) in order to work its way into conscious learning. From there, in order to be usable in any longer term sense, it has to be recreated and reinforced in relation to other new forms of information and experience through repeated practice. All of this has to be encoded and related to some positive sense of accomplishment and

Figure 11-8: *Coffee shops provide a template for a superior learning environment. There are a variety of seating options, the space usually has Wi-Fi access, facilitates learning individually, with a partner and with a small group, has a positive vibe and ambiance, serves food and beverages and usually has good acoustics and lighting.*

pleasure. Memorization, Willis argues, tends to stress recall rather than meaning, and recall tends to reside mainly in short-term memory, which has a very short half-life (around twenty minutes, she argues) (Willis 2006, 5ff). Teachers I have observed and interviewed often express frustration with how little of what they think they have taught is actually retained for any length of time by their students. It's hardly a mystery why this happens when most of the tasks I have observed involve either assimilating and repeating information in relatively short cycles, or "practice" at reproducing information on worksheets. In these instances, what children are "learning" is not the actual content but the practice of engaging and disengaging their short-term memory in repeated cycles.

This distinction between memory and learning is very practical. When I code teacher-student interactions in American classrooms, it turns out that something like 60-70% of the tasks that students are asked to do are memory and recall tasks. They consist of teachers asking students to do things and then asking them to perform tasks that demonstrate whether they remember how to do them. There are important variations in this pattern among schools and classrooms as well as internationally, but in the U.S. the functional definition of learning in classrooms turns out to be remembering and repeating stuff that the teacher or the textbooks have told you.

> Something like 60-70% of the tasks that students are asked to do are memory and recall tasks. They consist of teachers asking students to do things and then asking them to perform tasks that demonstrate whether they remember how to do them.

Another important distinction that arises from this definition is that learning is a highly individualized activity, heavily influenced by experience and practice over time. The complexity of this process cannot be captured by simple schematic input-output, or stimulus-response models, where a standard experience produces a reliable response on the part of the learner. Again, this is important to understand because a very high proportion of teacher-student interactions in U.S. classrooms assume that every student will assimilate a body of information in a more or less standardized way in the same amount of time. We routinely make judgments about the competence of students as learners by how well they meet specific learning goals on a standard timeline according to a standard model of "age-appropriate" expectations. The research on learning as a developmental activity does not support this view, but the bureaucratic necessities of schooling require it.

Finally, it shouldn't need to be said, but this definition of learning excludes the idea that learning is the simple transmission of information from one person to another. Learners are active agents in the reception and processing of information, not passive storage units. Their capabilities as learners depend crucially on the active development of strategies for integrating new information and experiences into existing understandings and prior learning experience.

The definition also tells us something about what learning is as well as what it is not. Learning is a cumulative developmental process that occurs over a life course. Central to this process is the concept of neuroplasticity. [7] It turns out that accomplished learners continue to develop neurologically — literally increasing, pruning, connecting, and elaborating networks of neurons into more efficient and powerful patterns — well into adulthood and old age. This process results in something neurologists elegantly call arborization, or the elaboration and integration of increasingly dense neural networks around highly specialized cognitive and affective functions. (My neurologist once complimented me, after an fMRI, for my "nice arborization." It made my day, whether true or not.) These processes look differently at different life stages — brain mass actually decreases, by a process called "pruning" — from adolescence into adulthood as we become more efficient at processing various types of

> Humans have had to overcome enormous physical disadvantages, relative to other species, in order to survive and develop. They have done so largely by compensating for physical limits with cognitive and social skills.

experience. The fundamental process of increasing neurological efficiency through practice and use is robust over a lifetime. In this sense, learning is a life practice, and humans make choices over a lifetime about the degree to which they engage in this practice. The cultivation of practice is central to the activity of learning. Practice is a lifetime project.

Learning is a biological and evolutionary necessity. Humans have evolved into learning organisms by engaging in activities that have caused increasingly complex forms of perception and cognition to develop. Humans have had to overcome enormous physical disadvantages, relative to other species, in order to survive and develop. They have done so largely by compensating for physical limits with cognitive and social skills. Most of this development has occurred as a result of direct experience through the deliberate activity of making and modifying our environment and the things in it. In this sense, learning is not something that occurs only in specific settings at specific times. It is a more or less continuous process growing out of physical necessity that occurs whether we choose to engage it or not.

Humans are distinctive among other species in their capability to consciously modify the ways they engage and experience their environment, and, in this sense, they can channel and manage learning in deliberate ways for specific purposes.[8] Humans are also special in that they are capable of developing conscious perception and understanding of themselves, their identities, and their capabilities as human actors. The parts of the brain that manage this process specialize in what neuroscientists call executive function. Highly developed executive function is a key marker of high capability as a learner. We have learned to use learning as a way of creating value, sustenance and pleasure, which means that deliberate, conscious pursuit of and control over learning can become self-reinforcing. We learn because it gives us pleasure, and the pleasure we experience from learning causes us to seek more learning. To the degree that we engage in activities that, intentionally or not, inhibit or discourage the pursuit of pleasurable learning, we are stalling and deflecting human evolution.

Learning is a somatic and tactile activity as well as a cognitive one. A major field of inquiry in the neuroscience of learning is embodied cognition,[9] which studies the relationship between the extended physiology of the body with the brain and its cognitive functions. A major finding of this research is that, in some as yet not fully understood way, we "think" not just with our brains but with our bodies in concert with our brains. In this sense, "experience" is not simply encoding and making sense of our perceptions in daily life, but also understanding how our ability to consciously engage and modify the environments we live in increases or inhibits our ability to learn and develop. Making and modifying things is a major way we "learn" through mind-body connections.

It should be clear by now that learning is a much broader activity, requiring and inviting a much broader definition of learning environments, than simply "doing school." One very useful metaphor that captures this idea is Alison Gopnik's wonderfully evocative distinction between the carpenter and the gardener (Gopnik 2017). Gopnik is a neuroscientist who studies learning in children from birth to age five — that is, before learning

> We have learned to use learning as a way of creating value, sustenance and pleasure, which means that deliberate, conscious pursuit of and control over learning can become self-reinforcing. We learn because it gives us pleasure.

becomes confounded with schooling. The findings of this body of research can only be described as amazing. She presents an inventory of the ways in which infants and preschoolers develop highly complex perceptual and cognitive capabilities that we have previously attributed only to adults. One astonishing finding, for example, is that children begin to develop something called a "theory of mind" — that is, the ability to distinguish between their own thoughts and the possible thoughts of others with whom they engage — as early as eighteen months of age, a faculty that had been previously identified with much later stages of development. We have failed to understand these important developmental patterns in large part because we have, in the past, relied heavily on research methods that require high levels of language development on the part of subjects. When you correct for this bias, it turns out that you find amazing neurological and cognitive complexity, including powerful capabilities for learning, in very young children that were previously attributed to adults.

Gopnik uses the metaphor of the carpenter and the gardener to frame the developmental project of human learning. Carpenters build to purpose and plan. Their materials are inert and must be combined and modified in order to produce a product. The results of their work are concrete and tangible objects that either function or not. If they don't function, they can be modified or built to a different plan. Gardeners, on the other hand, have to operate in partnership with nature in order to accomplish their goals. Their task is to understand, through study, observation, and practice, how live organisms live, grow, and adapt to often quite specific variations in their environment. Their results vary from one plant to the next, from one season to the next, and from one year to the next, often depending on imperfectly understood and complex interactions between plant and environment. Gopnik uses this metaphor to explain how viewing learning and development of children is trivialized and stunted by build-to-plan models of parenting and schooling, and how understanding infants and children as

Figure 11-9: *Learning is not the simple transmission of information from one person to another. Learners are active agents in the reception and processing of information, not passive storage units.*

resilient, competent, highly evolved learning organisms operating in a variety of environments can teach us how to build their capabilities as learners. This core idea of infants and children as learning organisms, of course, has a long history — Gopnik did not invent it. What is novel about Gopnik's approach is that it is backed by deep research on the actual neurological development that occurs as children evolve their capabilities as learners, and how consistent these patterns of development are with what we know about how human beings have evolved as a species.

Gopnik makes a particularly acerbic critique of "parenting" manuals that stress abstract models of child development and build-to-plan views of raising successful children. Her critique also extends to scripted instructional practices in schools and to highly structured, attainment-based models of learning. Gopnik's argument is a preview of a looming split between emerging research on the neuroscience of learning, on the one hand, and the existing conventional wisdom about standards, rigor, and relevance in American educational reform. Americans have never been particularly adept at incorporating serious scientific inquiry into the design of schools, and the growth of knowledge in the neuroscience of learning poses little or no short-term threat to schooling in the U.S., because neuroscientists are too busy doing research to develop models of clinical practice that threaten standard educational practice. Sooner or later, however, there will have to be some reckoning with or rejection of the emerging findings of the neuroscience of learning.

Here are a few principles that might begin to guide experiments in the design of future learning environments:

Human beings are learning organisms.

Millennia of human evolution have biologically programmed human beings to learn. In some basic sense, humans do not need to be "taught" how to learn. They are equipped to learn from birth. By age five or six, they have already mastered the two or three of the most complex cognitive and emotional developmental tasks humans confront — the development of language, the ability to differentiate themselves from others, and the ability to manipulate their human and material environment for purposeful ends. The job of adults, caregivers, and society at large is to engage with, to encourage, to support, and to develop this innate biological drive with sufficient curiosity and humility so as not to suppress and disable it. For better or worse, the real developmental work of learning — the complex project of learning how to become a competent and powerful learner in the world — must be done by the learner herself. We can construct environments that enable and support this work, we can populate these environments with people who have the competence and humility to model what powerful learning might look like, and we can exercise restraint in our own urges for custody, control, and judgment, but the work of turning curiosity into competence lies with the learner.

Figure 11-10: *Deliberate, conscious pursuit of and control over learning can become self-reinforcing. We learn because it gives us pleasure, and the pleasure we experience from learning causes us to seek more learning.*

A major lesson we have learned from attainment-driven models of schooling is that it is possible to disable human beings as learners by convincing them that they do not have the capability to manage their own learning. Attainment models require failure as a condition for success; models in which everyone is assumed to be competent in different ways at the same critical task called learning are considered to be flabby and to lack sufficient rigor, merit, and legitimacy. They are suspect because they challenge the existing distribution of privilege. The social costs of this model are horrendous. The question is whether those costs matter enough to open up the design of learning environments to more divergent thinking. The knowledge base is growing, the creativity exists, the future is uncertain. [10]

> A major lesson we have learned from attainment-driven models of schooling is that it is possible to disable human beings as learners by convincing them that they do not have the capability to manage their own learning.

Individual variability is the rule, standardization is the exception.

Accepting the reality that humans are learning organisms carries a formidable cost in terms of our existing models of learning and education. We have chosen to organize institutionalized learning around 19th century models of human development and capability. Organizational structures are deeply entrenched in age-grade theories of human development; assessment and clinical treatment models are based largely on psychometric techniques that assume a normal distribution, despite the existence of alternative modes of assessment and practice; policies dictate attendance and compliance measures that require participation in age-grade structures regardless of the value they add; physical structures mimic the architecture of custodial institutions. These structures and processes are so heavily institutionalized that they will not be transformed on any time scale that is consistent with the development of new knowledge about learning.

The solutions to this predicament, in the foreseeable future, lie in the development of existence proofs of learning organizations that switch the order of standardization and variability. Initial designs will have to take their point of departure from the assumption that individuals — children and adults — come to the learning project from different points of origin developmentally and experientially. It is possible to create a common culture of learning as building on individual differences in a common culture of commitment to learning, but that requires treating each learner as a project in human development, rather than treat children as if they were representatives of predictable age-grade groups.

Knowledge equals information plus affect plus cognition plus fluency.

The late Albert Shanker, a powerful spokesperson for teachers over his lifetime, was fond of saying: "I taught the content, but the students didn't learn it. Define the meaning of 'teach' in that sentence." Shanker's observation captures one of the fundamental problems with attainment-driven learning. Attainment-driven incentive structures

> The late Albert Shanker, a powerful spokesperson for teachers over his lifetime, was fond of saying: "I taught the content, but the students didn't learn it. Define the meaning of 'teach' in that sentence." Shanker's observation captures one of the fundamental problems with attainment-driven learning.

reward the accumulation of credit and memory-based performance, rather than the more complex neurological skills of self-organization, curiosity, executive function, and fluency through practice. The teachers I have worked with routinely use the term "information" as if it were the object of teaching, as in "I have only so much time to get the information across before I have to move on to the next topic." This largely unconscious trope suggests that learning is a process of absorbing discrete bits of information; students are like sponges with varying capacities for absorption; the "best" students are those who are quickest at absorbing and repeating on command the information that teachers impart.

In fact, fluent and powerful learners tend to be highly variable in their absorptive capacity, depending on how interested they are in the knowledge they confront, how the knowledge domain matches their previous experience as learners, and how well they can use the skills of their previous learning to solve the puzzles of acquiring new knowledge. A common complaint of undergraduate college and university faculty (and, I can attest, graduate faculty as well) is that their students seem not to have mastered the prerequisite content that is represented on their high school (and college) transcripts. Between three quarters and one quarter of the students who have completed the demanding "A through G" high school curriculum requirements for enrollment in California higher education institutions are required to take non-credit remedial courses to correct for the prerequisite knowledge they are supposed to have already mastered in high school [11] (California Legislative Analyst March 2017). Faculty at elite universities have begun to require students who have achieved high scores on Advanced Placement tests

Figure 11-11: *Teach like a Gardener and not like a Carpenter.
Riverside School, Ahmedabad, India.*

Figure 11-12: *It is possible to create a common culture of learning as building on individual differences in a common culture of commitment to learning, but that requires treating each learner as a project in human development, rather than treat children as if they were representatives of predictable age-grade groups.*

— which are supposed to carry college credit — to take entrance exams for basic course content in their disciplines before they will accept their scores. Clearly, there is a difference between ticking boxes on a prescribed curriculum and knowing stuff at even a modest level of fluency. Clearly, the expectation embedded in the attainment model that "good" students are equally knowledgeable across a broad collection of domains doesn't seem to hold for a substantial proportion of young people.

The obsessive focus on curriculum content and the transmission of information in the attainment model runs against the grain of what we increasingly know about how fluent and accomplished learners operate. They tend to follow their interests, often obsessively, in ways that educators find a bit scary. They are good at following cues that lead through successive layers of complexity in a given knowledge domain. They develop heuristics for deciding what is relevant, interesting, and useful information, based on schematic models of the knowledge domain they are working in. They cultivate the capacity to relate new information to their fund of existing knowledge. Most importantly, they are passionate about what they are learning. In other words, information becomes knowledge when it is captured by a learner who is affectively engaged and deliberate in the acquisition of fluency in a given domain. No one becomes a fluent learner in a field they find repellent. No one becomes a fluent learner following a script they had no role in creating.

There is a version of this model that can be described as brain chemistry — certain hormones and neurotransmitters are stimulated by engagement in certain kinds of activity, which lead to the engagement of cognitive capacity and the development of increasing complexity of neurons dedicated to the acquisition and processing of information in a given domain. (Damasio 2010, 67-94) You don't need to know the brain chemistry to know that highly motivated, fluent learners tend to be people who exercise deliberate control of their immediate learning environment, and for whom the pleasure of finding the next thing is the main source of their motivation.

> You don't need to know the brain chemistry to know that highly motivated, fluent learners tend to be people who exercise deliberate control of their immediate learning environment, and for whom the pleasure of finding the next thing is the main source of their motivation.

Depth and continuity over coverage.

A wise psychotherapist, Deborah Britzman, has described the experience of schooling as "an avalanche of certainties," a tsunami of answers to long-forgotten questions (Britzman 2009). I recall sitting in a high school chemistry class being lectured on Boyle's Law — that the pressure and volume of a gas are inverse to each other at a constant temperature — and thinking to myself, "how in the world did Boyle figure this out?" while other more disciplined students dutifully reproduced the formula and the teacher's explanation in their notebooks. The riveting story of an amateur scientist in the 17th century puzzling over a question few people had thought to ask would have been considered an unfortunate distraction for a beleaguered science teacher who was already a week behind the syllabus for the year. Most school-based science had, for me, this quality of "stuff to be memorized" with little or no reference to how the science came about or what scientists actually do. I did reasonably well in "advanced" science courses as a student, but I was unmotivated by answers to which there seemed to be no prior questions, or, more specifically, no human beings asking questions. I have since spent on the order of 150 hours or so observing, recording, and analyzing middle and high school math and science classrooms and what I observed accords with my own experience in school. More importantly it accords with aggregate data on American classrooms and with the observations of the practitioners I have worked with. There are, to be sure, exceptions — some of them spectacular examples of learning how scientists actually work and what mathematicians actually do. The exceptions are a tiny proportion of the total, and they prove the rule. Fine-grained observational studies across broad samples of classrooms confirm wide variability in levels of cognitive challenge from one setting to another, skewed significantly toward the less-challenging end of the distribution (Hill, Blazar, and Lynch 2015).

My own experience learning mathematics is instructive. Math was not my favorite subject, to say the least. Every math course I took after my freshman undergraduate year was always going to be the last math course I would ever take. But I was an uber attainment junky, which meant that I continued to take math courses through college into graduate school because to do so made me part of a privileged class of people thought

> Why did I have to wait until I was 27 years old, doing time in one increasingly obscure and terminally boring math class after another, to discover that math is a language that can be used to discover and describe the world?

11 CHAPTER THE CHALLENGES OF LEARNING AND DESIGN

> The brutal emphasis on content coverage inherent in the attainment model undercuts the more fundamental task of building capability and fluency in any useful domain.

Figure 11-13: *We have a lifetime to learn. The disposition to see the world in particular and useful ways is something that can only be learned through depth and practice, not by racing through a syllabus.*
Riverside School, Ahmedabad, India.

to be deserving of higher status. One day, when I was 27 years old, in graduate school at Harvard, I walked out of an econometrics lecture on some hopelessly obscure topic I can't recall, and I approached one of those incredibly complicated traffic intersections near Harvard Square. It suddenly occurred to me with an electric jolt, as I observed the drivers orchestrating their behavior through the intersection, that "math is everywhere!" I realized that I could actually build a model using the language of mathematics that would describe what I was seeing. Some years later another insight hit me with equal force: why did I have to wait until I was 27 years old, doing time in one increasingly obscure and terminally boring math class after another, to discover that math is a language that can be used to discover and describe the world? Virtually all the math I studied, because I had to, has receded into an obscure fog. What remains, for me, is a more or less fearless disposition to see the world through a series of frames, one of which is the language of mathematics. I could have learned that disposition in the early years of elementary school, in a decidedly different learning environment. Math, in my student world, was less a language for exploring and understanding the world than it was a way of culling the herd.

Our confounding of learning with course-taking, transcript-building, test-taking, and status-marking has led us away from a central insight of neuroscience, which is that human beings develop and build their capabilities to sense and understand the world through the acquisition of multiple "codes" or symbolic languages. We do this through exposure and practice, but, as my own example attests, simply being exposed to a broad range of languages doesn't mean that we learn how to use them to understand the world. In this sense the brutal emphasis on content coverage

Figure 11-14: *As learning begins to migrate out of institutions into the broader world, the challenge — and the promise — will increasingly be the creation of physical environments where young people want to be, rather than where they are required to be.*
Anne Frank Inspire Academy, San Antonio, Texas.

inherent in the attainment model undercuts the more fundamental task of building capability and fluency in any useful domain. We have a lifetime to learn. The disposition to see the world in particular and useful ways is something that can only be learned through depth and practice, not by racing through a syllabus. I would have become a much more engaged and competent mathematician if, at the age of five or six, I had been given a clipboard, a pencil, and sheet of paper and asked to go out and count something in the world that mattered to me and to explain what I saw and why it mattered. Not fancy enough for this hyper-institutionalized world in which the Common Core specifies something like twenty discrete math competencies that children should have mastered by age nine. [12]

Learning and Design: Hard Questions, Provisional Answers

Ambitious ventures in uncertain times begin with hard questions rather than clear answers. We are entering a period when, for better or worse, the meaning and practice of learning in society will be transformed. The problematical democratization of

> "The disposition to see the world in particular and useful ways is something that can only be learned through depth and practice.

11 CHAPTER THE CHALLENGES OF LEARNING AND DESIGN

Figure 11-15: *The practical and physical design challenges of building learning environments that incorporate the full range of human talents that learners bring are formidable, and they are not susceptible to simple prescriptions.*
Entry and Heart of School. Fisher STEAM Middle School, Greenville, South Carolina.
Photo by Kris Decker/Firewater Photography.

11 CHAPTER THE CHALLENGES OF LEARNING AND DESIGN

> If the cultivation of the practice of learning becomes the object of learning, rather than the accumulation of information and algorithms, what will formal learning look like at various life stages?

access to information through digital culture will not be domesticated through established institutions. That genie is out of the bottle. The monopolization of access to learning by established institutions cannot be sustained for long in a world where individuals will have access to the world's experts in any given domain of knowledge with a few keystrokes. The hard boundaries of credentialing embedded in the traditional attainment structure will not survive a world where learning is a lifetime project in which failures at one phase of life can stimulate transformations at later stages, and in which the knowledge and skill requirements for a productive life will change many times over the course of a generation. These dramatic changes remind one of the apocryphal Chinese curse, "May you live in interesting times." Interesting, indeed. But also exciting and promising.

Through the lens of learning, then, here are some hard questions that might shape our future discussions and projects around the design of learning environments:

How will humans adapt to transformations in the practice of learning?

If learning is the active creation, pruning, elaboration, and consolidation of neural networks, what will the practice of learning look like in the future? If "memory" of facts and information, algorithms and models, is a few keystrokes away in the digital cloud, how will the practice of learning change? If the cultivation of the practice of learning becomes the object of learning, rather than the accumulation of information and algorithms, what will formal learning look like at various life stages?

One clear implication of these questions is that the physical and cultural design of learning environments should accommodate more or less continuous adaptations to emerging knowledge and insights around the practice of learning. To reiterate an earlier theme, the project of designers and practitioners of learning is to make the familiar strange, to question how established structures and practices of learning influence, predetermine, and constrain what human beings think is possible, and how designs can encourage a disposition for surprise at what human beings are capable of doing. physical space as

11 CHAPTER THE CHALLENGES OF LEARNING AND DESIGN

Figure 11-16: *Exterior of Fisher STEAM Middle School, in Greenville South Carolina. Photo by Kris Decker/Firewater Photography.*

the site for thoughtful observation of learners at work; for reflection on the dispositions and competencies of individual learners; for learners to operate at different levels and trajectories in their development of the practice of learning; and for learners to tutor and coach each other in their practice.

How will the practice of learning and the design of learning environments adapt to the democratization of expertise?

However one might feel about it, the debate about the survival and ubiquity of **Wikipedia** is over; the arguments now revolve around how to sustain, monitor, and improve the medium as a self-organizing learning environment. **Wikipedia** is only one among thousands of examples of the emerging importance of self-organizing learning networks. If you are the parent of a middle-schooler struggling with how to factor a quadratic equation, at last count, you have a choice of several dozen different online teachers to correct for the limitations of your child's math teacher. The problem is no longer whether there are alternatives to institutionalized learning, but how to navigate and make use of them and how to correct for the inevitable social inequalities in access to them. Sometime in the next decade society will begin to question whether putting a group of children in an enclosed space with single adult who is the sole arbiter of what constitutes learning in a subject domain is a viable way to develop the learning competencies of **their** individual child.

As noted earlier, the movement of learning environments from hard, crystalline structures, based on narrow attainment-driven models of learning, through more fluid and flexible structures better adapted to individual differences, toward networked relationships that follow the contours of where expertise actually resides in society will be the central design challenge of the next decade or so. At the very least, learning environments will require more flexible and permeable physical and cultural boundaries, accommodating the movement of information and people.

How will society orchestrate its duty of care and responsibility for socialization of children and adolescents with the unfreezing of institutionalized learning?

Currently, society's answer to the role of schooling in duty of care and socialization is relatively straightforward: We legally require children and adolescents to spend something like 16,000 hours (more like 17,000-18,000 hours, counting homework and exam preparation) housed in a single physical setting under the (imperfect) custody and control of designated, credentialed adults. Underlying this arrangement is the imperfectly realized assumption that this enormous command of children's time and lives nurtures their cognitive and emotional development. This effective monopoly of custody and control is confounded with and legitimized by an authoritative attainment structure that is nominally charged with allocating privilege and merit in the larger society. It is possible that as learning begins to escape the bounds of this structure, its social authority will begin to erode. Because this structure is so deeply embedded in advanced capitalist society, it is far from clear that society has a Plan B for how it will adapt to the erosion of its authority.

A question that is central to the future design of learning environments and worth a great deal of thought and creativity is how to preserve the important elements of human connection and relationships that are central to the development of competent and accomplished learners. One painfully obvious response to this question is that learning environments have to be places where young people want to be — attractive, responsive, adaptive, comfortable spaces populated by people whose warmth and curiosity align with the dispositions of their clients. We know a great deal about how to design these environments; we obviously know a great deal less about how to move the enormous capital stock of institutionalized learning in the direction of creating such spaces. As learning begins to migrate out of institutions into the broader world, the challenge — and the promise — will increasingly be the creation of physical environments where young people want to be, rather than where they are required to be.

How will learning environments adapt to the challenges of individualization?

The neuroscience of learning and the social democratization of learning both point in the same direction: increasing adaptation of the form, content, and practices of learning to the individual differences of learners. In the theory, the hallmark of institutionalized learning has been equality, defined as universal access to prescribed content through an attainment structure based on objective measures of merit. The struggles to make this structure responsive to individual differences have been persistent and well-intentioned, as well as predictably ineffective. The more we know about learning, the less this structure makes sense in terms of both the individual's growth and development in the practice of learning and society's stakes in the creation of a broad-based vital and creative society and economy. It is less and less plausible that we will solve society's problems with a structure founded on the guaranteed failure and subordination of a large proportion of its young people.

The practical and physical design challenges of building learning environments that incorporate the full range of human talents that learners bring are formidable, and they are not susceptible to simple prescriptions. They will require the creation of: a culture of deep curiosity and inquiry about the capabilities of human beings as learning organisms; a culture characterized by its willingness to be surprised at the richness, variety, and resourcefulness of the human organism as a learning being; a culture less invested in making distinctions among more and less worthy individuals and more invested in the cultivation of individual interests and competencies — thus a culture of gardeners rather than carpenters. The physical settings for learning will have to adapt, for example, to what happens when learners outgrow the knowledge and competencies of their nominal teachers and tutors, what happens when a learner discovers a deep interest in a domain for which they have little prior preparation, what happens when learning jumps the boundaries of conventional content domains and challenges conventional curricula, what happens when a learner with serious physical limits in one neurological domain is discovered to have unusual competencies in another, and (heaven forbid) what happens when an otherwise competent and highly motivated learner becomes a listless and seemingly unmotivated learner. Just listing these few possibilities in a more or less limitless range of learning challenges helps us understand the appeal of highly institutionalized definitions of learning — they make the work much simpler. Frederick Engels is alleged to have said, "The problem with socialism is that it spoils too many good evenings at home." One could say the same about the problem of neuroscience and learning — energizing, but far from comfortable.

SOURCES

Britzman, Deborah. 2009. The Very Thought of Education: Psychoanalysis and the Impossible Professions. Albany, NY: State University of New York Press.

Claxton, Guy. 2015. Intelligence in the Flesh: Why Your Mind Needs Your Body Much More Than it Thinks. New Haven, CT: Yale University Press.

Damasio, Antonio. 2010. Self Comes to Mind: Constructing the Conscious Brain. New York: Random House/Vintage.

De Houwer, Jan, Barnes-Holmes, Dermot, and Moors, Agnes. "What is Learning? On the Nature and Merits of a Functional Definition of Learning." Psychonomic Bulletin Review, https://ppw.kuleuven.be/okp/_pdf/DeHouwer2013WILOT.pdf.

Ellis, Robert and Goodyear, Peter, eds. 2018. Spaces of Teaching and Learning: Integrating Perspectives on Research and Practice. Singapore: Springer.

Ellis, Robert, Goodyear, Peter, and Marmot, Alexi. 2018a. "Spaces of Teaching and Learning: An Orientation." In Ellis and Goodyear 2018, 1-12.

Ellis, Robert, Goodyear, Peter, and Marmot, Alexi. 2018b. "Learning Spaces Research: Framing Actionable Knowledge." In Ellis and Goodyear 2018, 221-238.

Elmore, Richard. 2018. "Design as Learning, Learning as Design." In Ellis and Goodyear 2018, 47-62.

Elmore, Richard. 2015-present. Leaders of Learning. An online course sponsored by Harvard X: https://www.edx.org/course/leaders-learning-harvardx-gse2x-2.

Gopnik, Alison. 2017. The Gardner and The Carpenter: What The New Science of Child Development Tells Us About the Relationship Between Children and Parents. New York: Farrar, Straus, and Giroux.

Hill, Heather, Blazer, Daniel and Lynch Kathleen. 2015. "Examining Personal and Institutional Predictors of High Quality Instruction." http://journals.sagepub.com/doi/full/10.1177/2332858415617703.

Honig, Meredith, ed. 2006. New Directions in Education Policy Implementation. Albany, NY: State University of New York Press.

11 CHAPTER THE CHALLENGES OF LEARNING AND DESIGN

Kaas, J.H. 2001. "Neural Plasticity." In International Encyclopedia of the Social and Behavioral Sciences. London: Elsevier. 10542-10546.

Kandel, Eric. 2006. <u>In Search of Memory: The Emergence of a New Science of Mind</u>. New York: Norton.

Katz, Mark. 2016. <u>Children Who Fail at School and Succeed in Life: Lessons from Lives Well-Lived</u>. New York: Norton.

Lakoff, George and Johnson, Mark. 1980/2003. Metaphors We Live By. Chicago: University of Chicago Press.

Legislative Analyst's Office, State of California. March 2017. Overview of Remedial Education at the State's Higher Education Segments. http://www.lao.ca.gov/handouts/education/2017/Overview-Remedial-Education-State-Public-Higher-Education-Segments-030117.pdf

National Research Council. 1997. Enhancing Organizational Performance. Washington, D.C. National Academies Press.

National Research Council. 2000. How People Learn: Brain, Mind, Experience, and School: Expanded Edition. Washington, DC: The National Academies Press.

Schacter, Daniel. 2001. The Seven Sins of Memory: How the Mind Forgets and Remembers. New York/Boston: Houghton Mifflin.

Senge, Peter. 1990/2006. The Fifth Discipline: The Art and Practice of the Learning Organization. New York: Doubleday.

Tyack, David, 1997. Tinkering Toward Utopia: A Century of Public School Reform. Cambridge, MA: Harvard University Press.

[1] Richard Elmore is Research Professor at the Graduate School of Education, Harvard University. richard_elmore@harvard.gse.edu.

[2] David Tyack analyzes the relationship between "reform" and what he characterizes as "the grammar" of schooling" — deeply embedded structures and norms — in Tyack 1997.

[3] For a review of research on the relationship between organizational form and environment, see National Research Council 1997, especially Chapter 1, "Organizational Change and Redesign," 11-38.

[4] This framework was originally developed for the Harvard X online course, Leaders of Learning. Elmore 2015-present.

[5] This is essentially what experts in the field of learning would call a "functional" definition, meaning that it stresses learning as manifest in changes in behavior over time. For a development of this view and its alternatives, see De Houwer, Barnes-Holmes, and Moors 2013.

[6] See, for example, Robert Bjork's lecture, "Forgetting as a Friend of Learning: Implications for Teaching and Self-Regulated Learning," October 13, 2013, Harvard Initiative for Learning and Teaching, https://hilt.harvard.edu/event/dr-robert-bjork-ucla.

[7] Kaas 2001 defines "neural plasticity" as the development and elaboration of connections among neighboring neurons in response to "events in the external environment," and as "essential for the normal development of the brain, creating the differences in those circuits that make us individuals."

[8] For a riveting account of how this human capacity for self-conscious growth and modification of cognitive and emotional capabilities has developed and evolved, see Damasio 2010.

[9] For an accessible discussion of the neuroscience of embodied cognition, see Claxton 2015.

[10] A remarkable demonstration of the costs of the attainment model and of the remarkable resilience of human beings who have "failed" in that model is Mark Katz's study of children who fail in school and succeed in adult life. (Katz 2016) Katz, a clinical psychologist, documents the range of strategies that his clients have developed to overcome the stigma of failure in school and develop their capacities as learners and as active agents in their own lives.

[11] The proportions are: three quarters of community college entrants, about 40 percent of state college entrants, and about one-quarter of entrants to the elite University of California campuses.

[12] see: http://www.corestandards.org/Math/Content/3/introduction/

ACKNOWLEDGEMENTS

PRAKASH NAIR

The publication of this book is an opportunity for me to look back at my unlikely, even seemingly impossible, life journey and thank all the amazing people who made it possible.

Here is a photo of me (standing on the right) as a 10-year-old with my brother Deepak heading to St. Patrick's High School in Secunderabad, India. A fairly typical Catholic School for middle class families, St. Pats crammed around 70 students into 500 SF classrooms and the teachers delighted in regular corporal punishment. Teaching was spotty at best but, in retrospect, that may have been the best thing to happen to us as learners who mostly had to fend for ourselves.

Strong friendships at school, a loving family at home, after-school activities like walking and playing with friends, cricket, climbing trees, swimming, the occasional James Bond movie, the Beatles and of course, the long, hot, lazy summers spent with every book I could lay my hands on, all combine to create a collage of memories that make my childhood a truly special time.

The one most obvious "theme" of my life are the people in it and the humble realization that none of us who has achieved anything in life can claim to be "self-made." I learned lessons of craftsmanship, attention to detail and innovative solutions to problems from my father. I remember my mother's kindness, her hugs and her organization skills and wonder how she found time to read to us in the midst of her crazy, busy life. My brother Deepak was my constant companion with the patience of a saint at my juvenile antics.

The next defining chapter was my architecture education in India, a wild adventure during which a whole new group of people, especially Vanitha, left their indelible imprint that continues to influence who I am today. Architecture also brought me to the United States and the list of my many mentors who guided me would be too long to list but Ed Kirkbride and his lovely wife Carole deserve special mention as do my friends Stu and Rose.

The person most responsible for placing me firmly on my current professional path that I have traversed for almost 20 years as an educational architect is my wife Jody who had more faith in me than I had in myself. There is no question at all that without her egging me on, I would still be a government bureaucrat in New York City. Mere words can hardly express my gratitude to her for everything she has done and for being the amazing, steadying force she has been.

My daughters Delta and Mallika make me proud for the wonderful people they have become and my son Jake with his sharp intellect is more a teacher to me than I have ever been to him. My love for them inspires everything I do. That reservoir of love extends to my grandson Asher whose infectious smile and creative energy rub off on me each time I see him.

ACKNOWLEDGEMENTS

Richard Elmore has been a huge source of inspiration to me for so many years now. His ideas have shaped my thinking and he has had a significant influence on my work. Richard has generously shared his ideas with me and worked with us on a number of projects such as the ones in Boulder Valley, Colorado. I'm truly grateful to Richard for agreeing to come on board as a co-author of this book.

Life is full of surprises and one of the nicest ones in mine is my talented co-author, Architect Roni Zimmer Doctori. This book was her idea and she is the one who proposed its Live | Play | Engage | Create structure. Roni is Wonder Woman! She is somehow able to juggle the demands of a big family with four children, an intense job that has her crisscrossing the length and breadth of the country, travel internationally to keep up with the various projects she is working on and still find time to work on this book and a whole range of new initiatives for FNI. I learn something new from her every day and am proud to call her my friend.

ACKNOWLEDGEMENTS

RONI ZIMMER DOCTORI

I would like to thank my parents Avner and Bella Zimmer, my first teachers, who laid the foundation for who I am today. With unlimited love and support, they empowered me with the freedom I needed, and the space to grow and thrive, to become the confident person I am today. My gratitude extends to my two sisters Adi and Anat, who were my first competitors and critics, who challenge me still and encourage me to dare, commit and invest in order to reap the results of personal satisfaction and pride that bind our loving family together.

I want to thank my husband and partner Meron, the father of our four children, who did everything in his power to support, encourage and assist me in writing this book. He was fully supportive of every effort required to enable me to progress professionally, and to learn and develop in new and exciting directions. More importantly, thank you Meron for being the wonderful dad that you are, guiding the way in and out of the house, taking the lead in every possible way. As the son of two teachers who has himself been teaching in different formats for many years, he "dragged" me away from being a tour guide, a fortuitous job that allowed us to cross paths for the first time, to a challenging and enjoyable experience as a teacher. That short stint in teaching provided me many insights that are still beneficial to me.

Thanks to my lovely children, Malachi, Lia, Daniel and Shira, who bring to my life a lot of light and joy, and from whom I learn every day, for 17 years now, how to be a good mother and a better person. Parenthood brings with it many blessings and great values that I hope to give back to my children so that they will grow up as independent thinkers, confident to take on the

ACKNOWLEDGEMENTS

world. My hope for them is that they will grow up to be good people, contribute to society and be loving parents to my future grandchildren who will continue the generational cycle of doing good in the world. Our love for those we hold most cherished in our hearts makes us exert ourselves to constantly try to be better than we are. I love each one of them very much and this love has been a big driving force in my life.

On the professional and personal side, I would like to thank architect Monika Glait who was the first to draw me into school design work for being a dedicated and patient teacher to me. I appreciate and cherish her professional abilities, the knowledge and experience she has accumulated during her many years of work and the constant smile and joy she always brings with her.

I would also like to thank Koby Bogin, CEO of ABT Planners, and Danny Keidar, who heads the office in the Jordan Valley, for making ABT an incubator for personal growth and for letting me choose the direction for my professional development. They monitored with interest every step I made, showed great patience and always offered me support in every way they could. Thanks to them, I was able to maintain professional cooperation with FNI within the protective and comfortable umbrella of a large, nationally renowned and well-established architectural firm.

Last, but certainly not the least, I am deeply grateful to Prakash Nair, my partner in writing this book who, over the course of the work we have done together, became not only a professional colleague but a good friend as well. Although we come from different and seemingly alien worlds, Prakash and I have found, along the way, many areas of synergy that have enabled us to have a fascinating and empowering connection. Despite the differences in background, language and culture and the geographical distance that separates us, it was very easy for me to connect to the great heart of this generous and impressive man and his special spirit. A spirit that cast a light over me and was strong enough to make me fly to new heights as well.

Finally, I would like to thank all the good, smart and interesting people I met and worked with during the fascinating professional journey of writing this book and during the formative years that led me to this special place in my life and career. In the Mishnah (Avot 4: 1) it is said: "Who is the wise? One who learns from every person." I am learning new and fascinating things every day from all those wonderful men and women whom destiny, and perhaps a guiding hand, have brought into my life. Learning from each other is one of the most enjoyable ways to learn. To me, constant, never-ending learning is the essence of life itself. Learn, grow and do good in our world. I think it is what we are all here for. My work on this book was driven by this spirit of wanting to contribute my little share of goodness while never ceasing to be a curious learner.

RICHARD ELMORE

I would like to thank, first, Darrell Fraser, former Deputy Secretary of the Victoria Department of Education and Early Childhood Development, Victoria, Australia, for introducing me to the amazingly creative and deeply knowledgeable educators and architects who created some of the most beautiful and innovative learning environments in the world, and whose leadership made this burst of creativity possible. Thank you also to Prakash Nair and the astonishingly creative talent at Fielding/Nair for allowing me to tag along on some of their important, innovative projects to learn about the fascinating connection between learning and physical design. Finally, I was given enormous latitude and unparalleled creative support by the team at Harvard X to develop the online course, Leaders of Learning, that resulted in the Modes of Learning framework— especially Sarah Grafman, whose special gifts made me look much better than I actually am.

ABOUT THE AUTHORS

PRAKASH NAIR

Prakash Nair is a futurist, a visionary architect and the Founding President & CEO of Education Design International, one of the world's leading change agents in school design with consultations in 52 countries on six continents. He is the recipient of many international awards including the A4LE MacConnell Award, the highest honor worldwide for school design.

He has written extensively in leading international journals about school design and educational technology and their connection to established educational research. He has written two books including the landmark publication, *The Language of School Design*, and *Blueprint for Tomorrow: Redesigning Schools for Student-Centered Learning* published by Harvard Education Press.

Prakash served as an instructor for Harvard edX "Leaders of Learning," an online course with 190,000 enrolled which lets you explore and understand your own theories of learning and leadership. Led by Harvard's Dr. Richard Elmore, Leaders of Learning helps identify and develop educators' personal theory of learning and explore how it fits into the shifting landscape of learning.

Prakash worked for 10 years as Director of Operations for a multibillion-dollar school construction program for New York City. Over the past 20 years, he has served as a Managing Principal on several projects scattered around the world. His signature talent lies in his ability to communicate his passion for a new approach to education across the globe. He forges strong partnerships with local firms, helps client communities visualize their futures, builds consensus for uniquely tailored solutions, and helps execute them successfully.

Contact Prakash Nair at Prakash@EducationDesign.com

ABOUT THE AUTHORS

RONI ZIMMER DOCTORI

Roni is a Principal Architect with Education Design Intenrational and represents a new generation of visionary young architects who understand the profound ways in which the built environment impacts student learning outcomes. She has over 17 years of professional architectural and project management experience. She has served as an Architect and Design Team Leader at AlefBet Planners in Israel since 2007.

Roni has lectured, conducted workshops, presented keynote conference talks and delivered a full day Masterclass on school design in deffernet parts of the world including Australia and Canada. Her portfolio of educational work includes various schools throughout Israel. For the past three years, Roni has collaborated on innovative educational projects including the nationally renowned GOGYA Teacher Training Academy developed by the AMIT Network of Schools. During this time, she has travelled to/worked on projects in Australia, Canada, India, Romania, Singapore, Spain, Switzerland, Thailand, Timor Leste and teh United States.

Roni has extensive knowledge of and experience working on a variety of projects including public buildings, welfare and community buildings, tourism and leisure complexes, neighborhoods and residential buildings, industrial and office buildings. She graduated with honors from the Faculty of Architecture and Town Planning, Technion – Israel Institute of Technology, in Haifa.

Roni's commitment to education is inspired by the schooling experience of her own children. She represents a new generation of visionary young architects who understand the profound ways in which the built environment impacts student learning outcomes.

She believes passionately that there is an urgent imperative for education change in Israel and throughout the world so that students are better prepared for a very different future than anything we have seen before. Towards this goal, Roni has been working closely with EDI's President Prakash Nair and other senior managers at the Company to explore a wide range of effective education solutions. These include not just new ways to design school buildings but also methods to introduce and implement highly innovative, student-centered curriculums in new and renovated schools.

Contact Roni Zimmer Doctori at Roni@EducationDesign.com

DR. RICHARD ELMORE

Richard Elmore joined the faculty of the Harvard Graduate School of Education in 1990, having previously taught at the College of Education, Michigan State University, and the Graduate School of Public Affairs, University of Washington. He is a member of the National Academy of Education, and a past president of the Association for Public Policy and Management, the national organization representing graduate programs in public policy and management. He has held positions in the federal government as a legislative liaison with the U.S. Congress on education policy issues. He is currently director of the Doctor in Educational Leadership (Ed.L.D.) program at HGSE. His current research and clinical work focuses on building capacity for instructional improvement in low-performing schools. He spends at least one day per week in schools, working with teachers and administrators on instructional improvement. He is coauthor of Instructional Rounds in Education: A Network Approach to Improving Teaching and Learning (Harvard Education Press, 2009) and author of School Reform From the Inside Out: Policy, Practice, and Performance (Harvard Education Press, 2004).

Dr. Elmore is exploring how schools of different types and in different policy contexts develop a sense of accountability and a capacity to deliver high-quality instruction. He has also researched educational choice, school restructuring, and how changes in teaching and learning affect school organization.

ABOUT THE AUTHORS

DR. HEIDI HAYES JACOBS

Dr. Heidi Hayes Jacobs is founder and president of the Curriculum Designers Group, providing professional services to schools and organizations internationally to upgrade curriculum and support teaching strategies to meet the needs of 21st century learners. Dr. Jacobs' models on curriculum mapping and curriculum design have been featured in her 11 books and are the basis for software solutions used throughout the world.

Working with a range of organizations, Jacobs has online courses with PBS Teacherline and PD360 and has consulted to groups ranging from international, national, state and provincial education departments, professional organizations such as ASCD, NAESP, Learning Forward, the European Council of International Schools, the Near East School Association, the College Board, ADK International Sino-Canadian Schools in China, New Zealand's Learning Network, the Kennedy Center, the Peace Corps World Wise Schools, Carnegie Hall, Australia's EduTech,, and the United Nations Council on Teaching about the UN, the Near East School Association, the International Baccalaureate, the NY State Higher Education Commission, the CCSSO workgroup on Global Competencies, and AASA's Collaborative Project focused on innovation. In 2014 she received the MAIS International Educator Award in Seville, Spain. Dr. Jacobs is serving as program development advisor to Amazon Studios' children's programming division.

Dr. Jacobs' most recent book, Active Literacy: Active Literacy Across the Curriculum: Connecting Print Literacy with Digital, Media, and Global Competence, K-12, was released by Routledge in October 2017. Her book, co-authored with Marie Alcock, Bold Moves for Schools: How We Create Remarkable Learning Environments, was published by ASCD in 2017. Her recent four book series on Leading the New Literacies, Mastering Digital Literacy, Mastering Media Literacy, and Mastering Global Literacy were released in 2014 by Solution-Tree. Her bestselling books, Curriculum Mapping: Tools and Templates and Curriculum 21, both with ASCD, have been the basis for a wide range of professional services provided by a talented faculty and a robust clearinghouse giving educators resources to upgrade classroom life. Her education career began as a high school, junior high, and elementary teacher in Utah, Massachusetts and New York.

DESIGN CREDITS

A majority of the schools featured in this book were led by Prakash Nair, AIA while he served as President & CEO of Fielding Nair International which was reorganized in 2019. Prakash Nair now serves as President & CEO of Education Design International. Learn more about these projects at EducationDesign.com.

Shorecrest Prep School, Early Childhood Center, St.Petersburg, Florida, USA
Meadowlark School, Erie, Colorado. Boulder Valley School District, Colorado, USA
Centaurus High School. Boulder Valley School District, Colorado, USA
Hillel School of Tampa, Florida, USA
Academy of the Holy Names, Tampa, Florida, USA
Kevin Bartlett High School, International School of Brussels, Belgium
American School of Bombay, Mumbai, India
PK Yonge Developmental Research School at the University of Florida, Gainesville, USA
Summit Middle School. Boulder Valley School District. Colorado, USA
Anne Frank Inspire Academy, San Antonio, Texas, USA
Hillel School of Detroit, Michigan, USA
Norma Rose Point School, Vancouver, Canada
International School of Dusseldorf, Germany
High School for Recording Arts, St. Paul, Minneapolis, USA
Bloomfield Hills High School, Michigan, USA
Creekside Elementary School. Boulder Valley School District, Colorado, USA
Col.legi Montserrat, Barcelona, Spain
VEGA School, New Delhi, India
American Embassy School, New Delhi, India
Yew Chung International School of Chongqing. China
Horace Greeley High School, Chappaqua, New York
Singapore American School, Singapore
Emerald School. Boulder Valley School District, Colorado, USA
Ballarat Grammar School. Victoria, Australia
GOGYA Professional Development Center. Ra'anana, Israel
Fisher STEAM Middle School, Greenville, South Carolina, USA